FORGET REGRET

*A Memoir of Embracing Transformation
after a Traumatic Brain Injury*

Kamya Rilling

Pownal Street Press
CHARLOTTETOWN

Forget Regret: A Memoir of Embracing Transformation After a Traumatic Brain Injury. Copyright © 2025 by Kamya Rilling

All rights reserved. No part of this book may be reproduced, stored in a retrieval system or transmitted, in any form or by any means, without the prior written permission of the author except in the case of brief quotations embodied in reviews.

Requests for permission to make copies of any part of the work should be emailed to permissions at hello@pownalstreetpress.com. Our books may be purchased for promotional, educational, or business use. Please contact your local bookseller or Pownal Street Press to purchase.

Pownal Street Press · www.pownalstreetpress.com

Cataloguing data available from Library and Archives Canada

ISBN 978-1-998129-37-9 · Ebook ISBN 978-1-998129-38-6

Edited by Maureen Duffy · Copyedited by Alison Strumberger · Designed by Jordan Beaulieu

The information contained herein does not constitute medical/legal/etc. advice and neither PSP nor the author are legally responsible for any outcomes as a result of the opinions or information presented in the book.

Pownal Street Press gratefully acknowledges Mi'kma'ki, the ancestral and unceded territory of the Mi'kmaq First Nation on whose land our office is located.

Dedicated to my mother,
for everything she has done for me

Author's Note

While reading this story, please understand that I have written of my experience at the time, and not necessarily how I see life now or exactly how it happened. This story is about my learning process and how it changed me during a crucial time. Some events in this book are based on stories told to me, which I then reimagined to fit my own dialogue.

This story includes small but relevant discussions on some topics that may be disturbing to some individuals, including, but not limited to, addiction, religion, racism, mental health, mental disorders, domestic emotional abuse, and suicide.

Chapter One: The Accident

Sun shines through the window and warms my back. The smell of cedar fills my head with memories of the past and hope for the future. It's June 2009 and I am sixteen. At my summer job, I'm glueing little wooden wheels onto little wooden cars. Making toys is my favourite part of my job at The Toy Factory in New Glasgow, PEI. An errant wave of blonde hair, tinged red in the sunlight, falls in front of my face. Pushing it away, I meditate as I put glue in the holes of two wheels and hammer an axle into one. Threading the axle through the tiny chassis, I beat it into the second wheel. I roll to test, almost letting it drive off the table.

It's funny how fast time goes by. I'm one year away from graduating high school and enjoying my young, vibrant life. I have a sense that I am young and vibrant. People always talk about loving their jobs, and I know they're talking about careers, but why isn't it also important to love your summer job as a teenager? At least now I know what it feels like to love working while being compensated.

"Kamya, you're done for the day! Get out of here!" My boss, Karen, says, bringing me out of my dreamlike state. "You probably get your focus from your grandfather. He loved making toys too, didn't he?" I nod. My grampie used to make wooden toys in his basement when I was growing up. I remember sitting with him in his workshop and listening to his stories. He's the reason I got this job; he used to sell the surplus of his toys to the store. So, when I was thirteen and looking for my first official job, I came here to this family-owned toy shop to both make and sell toys. They hired me on the spot with nothing but babysitting on my resume and the knowledge that I was his granddaughter. I was very grateful.

The beautiful team at The Toy Factory welcomed me into their family, and moments like this, chatting with Karen about my grampie at the end of my shift, make me genuinely love living in the small province of Prince Edward Island, Canada. I have a wonderful family, and I love being connected to that.

"It's kind of an unusual day," I say as I move to stand with her at the workbench while I wait for my ride. "A couple of friends are coming to pick me up instead of Mom or Grammie, and we're going to town for our friend's father's wake. His son is a classmate of mine."

"Oh! Is that the man I heard died not too far from here in that awful accident? That is such a terrible story! His kids are so young," says Karen.

"Yep, that's him." I laugh a little. Everyone knows everything that happens around here. "It's amazing how fast life can change…" I trail off, look down and add, "I can't even imagine what it would be like to lose one of my parents. I depend on my mom so much, and even with my dad living in the States, he still calls daily to talk to me. It would be such a huge change."

Karen is quiet for a minute before changing the subject. "When do you get your license?" I'm one of the last of my friends to get their license. I get around fine, but I also can't wait for that sense of independence.

"Hopefully soon! I've got my learner's permit now and I've been doing lots of practice. For now, my friends don't mind driving me around, and it's not like I have a car. But it's something I can save towards."

I see my friends Kristy and Hanna pull up out front and say a quick goodbye to Karen as I fly out the door. In the car, I spin off the conversation with my boss. We start talking about the horrors of losing a parent, and how it is so important for us to go and show our support. When we arrive at the funeral home, there is a room filled with people we barely know. We give our love, offer condolences, and move along to avoid holding the line.

"I always hate the setup of wakes," I say as we head back into the car. "I think it's a great idea, but you never really get to have a good enough chat with the people there, and I always feel like I want to."

Both of my friends agree. Growing up in a small place like PEI, we all want to be there for each other, but so does everyone else. This is one of the reasons why a wake, especially here, is such an important tradition. As a result, the family can get time to be together and begin moving forward. A wave of sadness washes over me as I think of how difficult closure is to achieve.

Thank God, Kristy chimes into my thoughts, probably sensing that the wake had put us all in a slump. "I'm hungry and don't have time to eat when I get home. Do you guys mind if we make a stop at Wendy's to get a salad or something?"

"Sure! I'm definitely up for that," I say, immediately torn with guilt between a salad and a hamburger. I may be healthy enough now, but I'm getting older and it's time to start making more responsible decisions. I just better be rewarded for it, I swear.

We go through the drive-thru for our salads and wait for what seems like forever to pull out of the parking lot, through traffic, and back home. We're all getting antsy, but then Kristy finally spots an opening.

Sitting behind her, I look to my left. Content, I sit back and think about what I'll do when I get home—maybe I'll make a plate of nachos to make up for this salad and watch *Fresh Prince* reruns. I'm happy I work the day shift and don't need to rush off to work this evening.

Kristy takes her chance and pulls out into traffic.

I look up, and as if in slow motion, I suddenly feel my car door smash against my body. Glass sprinkles everywhere, like snow on an icy day. The door slices into my knee, crushes my hip and abdomen, and cuts across my face.

* * *

I hear a hissing sound, and people yelling at each other in the distance. I hear the squealing of brakes, then the sirens in the distance. I don't know what's real. Someone tries to open my door but they can't; the door has crumpled into me. Finally, I'm freed from the car. Pain carves through my body, but I can't identify where it's coming from.

People are all around me, and I'm quickly placed in an ambulance and the doors slam behind me. The chaos quiets. I hear a familiar voice, but I don't know whose. Still, it's comforting. My vision is sharp as I try to open my eyes—I can make out the figures in front of me but they aren't registering. I don't understand what's happening right now. I'm so tired I rest my eyes.

Chapter Two: The Coma

Due to a traumatic brain injury (TBI), I'm put into an induced coma in Charlottetown, then transferred to a hospital in Moncton, New Brunswick. The coma is supposed to take some pressure off my brain so things can settle down and start healing. Now that we're here, I'm where I need to be. For now, they're doing tests to learn what they can about the progress of my condition.

Once settled, my mother and brother, James, sit together in my hospital room, waiting for me to come back from some tests. Dad and Grammie are on their way. With Dad living in the States, he may take a day or two to get here. While my mom's mom lives very close to us, she would have let Mom and James come here first so that they could get settled before she joins us. Mom sits with a blank notebook with a neon-orange cover in her lap, which she uses to track my recovery. With her curly spiced-brown hair motionless in a quiet space, she writes out a list of my doctors' names, general injuries, and what medications I'm currently using, including ones for pain and sleeping. On the blank cover page that shows through the plastic cover, she slowly writes, *While You Were Sleeping*.

James is pacing. He goes and buys me a small stuffed dragon in the gift shop to lighten the mood. He places it near my hand, just in case I can feel it there. Staring at this little green dragon, with his chest puffed out in confidence, Mom reflects on when I was younger. She picks it up, squeezes it, and decides it's a great size for my small hands. A dinosaur might have been better since dinosaurs have been a popular token around my house lately, but you get what you get.

This past spring, after months of convincing, Mom let me foster a dog from the Humane Society. She can complain to me all she wants, but she was the one who chose the "pregnant stray" option on the foster form. The stray Border Collie gave birth to eight puppies in our basement. We separated Littlefoot from the rest of the litter at five weeks because he was diagnosed with megaoesophagus and couldn't get enough milk from his mother. He was named Littlefoot because of his stunted growth, which was due to his not getting an adequate amount of nutrition early in life. Littlefoot is a character from the film *The Land Before Time*, which was one my brother and I loved when we were kids, so it was the first name that came to mind. We moved him upstairs for Mom to feed him properly, and of course, she got attached. So, yes, a dinosaur would have been better, especially since Littlefoot couldn't be here, but dragons are good too, and dragons are magic. Maybe magic is just what we need right now. Returning to the notebook, Mom begins with the date and writes her first journal entry.

* * *

June 22, 2009

She starts with a simplistic explanation of my condition. I have a bruise in the right-middle part of my brain that's causing some paralysis on the left side of my body—my left arm is affected too and is responding slowly. That's all we know for now, anyway.

Fractures in the bones in her face, collarbone, and pelvis. Lacerations on spleen, left side of liver, left kidney. Broken ribs and a punctured lung. Tube in chest for drainage. A catheter has been inserted.

The neurosurgeon, Dr. Meadows, shaves the top of my head and positions a probe to monitor the swelling in my brain. The shaved part is above my forehead, where everyone can see it. I know Mom is probably laughing at that, thinking of what kind of reaction I'll have when I see it. I'm wearing compression socks to help with circulation, and I'm on a ventilator just in case, but I can breathe a little independently. My haemoglobin is good, so I shouldn't need more transfusions.

Cerebral Profusion Pressure (CPP) levels are good. Between the high 120s and low 130s. Blood Pressure (BP) and Heart Rate (HR) are average.

June 23, 2009

With my punctured lung, they have to monitor things carefully. They're testing for infection. I've had x-rays on my legs, pelvis, and back. My spinal cord is in good shape, although there is significant bruising on my back. A deep laceration in my leg has been stitched, and there's bruising on my left shin and hip area.

A facial x-ray confirms where the fractures are in my left cheek and that my skull wasn't damaged. BP and HR are still average. The unit doctor, Dr. Parker, says that the internal injuries are doing well at this time, so there is no need for surgery. My pelvis has a tiny fracture that will heal on its own, and it shouldn't prevent me from being able to walk again. All other injuries except for the brain should heal on their own in time, and I've got nothing but time.

The brain won't be able to recover like the rest, Mom is told. Neurons don't just sprout up like grass after a fire. What does that mean for me, when I wake up? The brain injury may be responsible for the limited motor function in my left arm. The bleed in my brain will be a waiting game for now, since they'll only be able to measure its effects after I wake up. The doctors tell Mom that I'm still young and growing, though, and my chances of recovery are good. The best treatment is to keep me sedated and allow my brain to heal. They say anywhere from forty-eight hours to three or five days. There's no harm in keeping me in an induced coma, but I'll need to stay on a ventilator, which can add the risk of pneumonia. The doctors and nurses will monitor this, and they'll continue to give me my medication for asthma and will continue to practice physical therapy on my lungs, chest, and limbs.

Finally, Mom gets off the serious stuff.

Today you had lots of visitors. James, Grammie and your great aunt, Aunt Amelia and Uncle Zack, and your Aunt Izzy and cousin Kiara are all here. James and Littlefoot will stay with your cousin Theodore while you are here, since it's close by.

Mom doesn't need to explain why Littlefoot can't just be left home on PEI like our other dog, a chocolate lab named Lindor. With Littlefoot's megaoesophagus, he needs to eat in a certain way, and so far, only Mom, James, and I know how to feed him. He eats vertically: we lift him, set him in a chair with a harness and leave him upright for 45 minutes to an hour while the food drops to his stomach with the help of gravity—otherwise he would just regurgitate it.

Kristy's mom called. Kristy is doing fine, but she's been asking about you and she's very concerned. James picked out a card for her, and Aunt Izzy will bring it back to her when she returns to the Island.

Later, after everybody else has left, Mom sits in an empty room with her daughter attached to tubes. The soft beeping of machines confirms to her that I am okay. Her eyes droop as she returns to the notebook.

I stayed with you until midnight. Around 11:30, nurses came in to reposition you, which you didn't like, and guess what? You lifted your left arm! Terrific.

June 24, 2009

You had a great night. BP and HR are good. Your CPP was under 20 all night, all on your own without medication. The nurses came in to draw blood and to wash your mouth out. It was obvious that you didn't like your mouth being opened and cleaned! But it did the job! You showed your disgust by lifting and moving your left arm! Not to mention squeezing my hand with your right hand with brute force. It's obvious your magical dragon did his job overnight. The swelling in your face has started coming down.

Mom records that I had lots of visitors again today. Dad and my stepmom came up from Vermont and were in today, plus James and Grammie. Aunt Izzy came back over the Confederation Bridge with some homemade North Shore lobster salad. Uncle Dale is a lobster fisherman, and Aunt Izzy knew everyone in the hospital would love a little treat.

"We promise to save you some, darling," Mom says as they eat it. Besides visitors, the nurses won't be doing significant tests today, so things are quieter. My physiotherapist comes in to do some work on my lungs and chest. She also does exercises on my arms and legs to help with blood flow and to keep them in motion. With Aunt Izzy's help, my hair is tamed and braided.

> *Kristy's mom called again. Kristy grabbed the phone to say hi, and thanked me for the card I sent. Kristy's mom mentioned that some of your friends are trying to organize a visit, but I told her it might be better to wait a little more time—right now, only family is allowed to visit. The moms both agree that you need your rest.*

> *2:30 pm. I left the room to use the washroom. Whenever I leave, I always ensure that Mr. Dragon takes the place of my hand. The poor thing, I think you've strangled him a few times.*

> *Oops, Mr. Dragon just fell to the floor. Maybe the nurse didn't see him? It's okay; I picked him up, and he's safe in my lap until they finish your check-up. XO*

June 24, 2009

> *A urologist came in today. She says your left kidney is healing, so there is no need for surgery. What a relief! This is great news. Another check in six weeks is needed to be sure the kidney is fully healed. Also, Dr. Meadows was in and he's very pleased with your progress. Your CPP, BP, and HP all did well overnight without requiring Mannitol to*

increase pressure. He wants to continue the medication that's keeping you in your coma until, hopefully, Friday to give your brain more quiet time. Unless, of course, you decide otherwise, and you want to wake up sooner? He says we will be here for at least another week. I miss you Kamya, but we're going to get through this—together.

James finally discovers the notebook. He makes a few quick edits in Mom's notes, then draws a small comic for me of my magical dragon on the front cover and then adds a message of his own:

Once I realized that stories were being recorded here, I decided to start writing them too, so you would at least have something interesting to read when you wake up! First, the dragon Mom keeps referring to is not Mr. Dragon, but "Agent D." Obviously it has to be a "Phineas and Ferb" themed name! His full name is Dragi the Dragon. To clarify, he is a secret agent. His duties are written on a paper to keep the nurses informed. Sure, he has some magical powers, but he also uses other non-magical skills to protect our greatest asset. The nurses all know that you like to hold Agent D and check the floor to see if he has fallen.

It's maybe a bit presumptuous to assume nurses have time in their day to check for a dropped toy for a sixteen-year-old in a coma, but they've all been very good to me since I came in. I wonder if it's because I'm so helpless.

Cousin Kiara and I got some CDs to play in your room. I don't know if you can hear music right now, but I play it in case you can. We have Regina Spektor, Coldplay, and Jack Johnson. Jack Johnson is the one who sang that Curious George song "Upside Down" that goes like, "Upside down do do do do olooolo do do do do."

Even when I'm in a coma, James manages to say things that would make me laugh. Since arriving, James continues to lighten the mood. I'm grateful he decided not to share how beaten up I must look. Instead, he tells me more about the compression socks I'm wearing.

By the way, you have these things on your feet, and they're basically the most intense socks I've ever seen. I am heading home tonight to bring Lindor in to keep Littlefoot company! I'll also visit Kristy for you tomorrow and say hi for you!

Grammie must have seen James writing in the notebook, because the following message is from her:

Wednesday Evening. I spent the day here to be close to you. You are doing so well, and your hands feel warm even as I hold them. I can feel the Irish strength you are displaying. Of course, Grampie is beside you, holding you close and, I'm sure, telling you to be strong and carry on. I love you so much and am so proud of you. I'm with you each moment as I hold you close in my thoughts and prayers, Grammie.

Her words remind me of summer days when I would run down the hill, through the field, to visit them. She always had such a luscious garden to play in with Grampie's little dog. There'd be a table in the kitchen where I could sit with Grampie and talk about various birds outside the window. Grampie would tell me stories upon stories while Grammie made us something delicious to eat.

Mom is back in the notebook late into the night to add some last words for the day:

I stayed with you until 11:30. The nurses gave you a sponge bath and used all the nice smelly things Aunt Izzy bought. You smell delicious now. You didn't like getting moved when they were making your bed, but you settled down after a while. They told me you were aggressive—hmmm, all those muscles from carrying Littlefoot have paid off. Force to be reckoned with, I told them. Good night, my girl. Xoxo.

June 25, 2009

I was here at 5:00 to say good morning. You had a good night and rested well. You now have one stuffed puppy on the left side of the bed and Agent D constantly in your right hand. Even though he's a perfect fit for your hand, Agent D can't breathe at times because you squeeze so tightly with your right hand. But don't worry! He's magical. He can take it. Today is the day they do another CT scan to see how your insides are healing. Your stomach was a bit swollen yesterday, but it seems better now. X-ray results came back, and your lungs look terrific. Your occupational therapist arrives today to work on your feet. They are starting to get weak from you just lying here, so she thinks putting on some shoes may help! Hopefully, they won't be as "intense" as the socks. Stay tuned!

Aunt Izzy stayed in the hostel with me last night. She gave me her makeup remover pads to try to get your mascara off, which was basically caked on you since it hasn't been washed off since you got here. You're all cleaned up and beautiful now. Your CT scan returned, and you're recovering well, with no indication or concern for infection.

The anaesthesiologist, Dr. Thornton, was just in to make some adjustments to your medications and to decide when to start feeding you again since the stomach tube was making you bloat. Haemoglobin is 112, which is stable. This proves there is no more internal bleeding, which is fantastic! BP 140/94, HR 92, CPP 74-11. Your father, stepmom, Grammie, and aunts Kye and Izzy are here today.

James adds, *And me!* He's always here, so that may be why Mom keeps forgetting him.

1:30 pm. Physio is here to do your exercises.

I get physiotherapy every day to stay as mobile as possible. Physio is done every day on my right lung. My neurosurgeon, Dr. Meadows, gives my mom a thumbs up on my progress and tells her they'll start taking me off the medication slowly, keeping me in the coma until I wake up on my own. Mom writes that it should happen either Saturday or Sunday, depending on my reaction and ability to stay calm and understand where I am.

Dr. Meadows said your CPP levels are doing great, and he's very pleased. However, we need to take things ONE DAY AT A TIME.

5:30 pm. BP 124/104, HR 102, CPP 102-16. Maggie, the nurse, did a nice job braiding your hair today. I can't wait to have your hair washed and done with your new shampoo. You're my greatest priority still. We're all here for you!

6:15 pm. BP 125/108, HP 108, CPP 70-11. We received a beautiful basket full of chocolates and goodies from my work. I think the raspberry chocolate is yours. Whose idea was that? You know how I feel about raspberries—they are certainly meant for either you or James.

> *7:00 pm. The unit doctor, Dr. Parker, was in to chat about your CT scan. Everything's looking good. He's going to try to change your chest tube tomorrow. Dr. Thornton will give you antibiotics right away. You only have a fever of 38.9, but just in case.*
>
> *You would like Dr. Thornton. He's British and weird, but all the nurses say he's brilliant, and guess what?? He flies his own plane! So cool!!! He calls you Baby Girl. Whenever he comes in, he says, "How's my baby girl doing?" Maggie is gone now, but Georgia is on instead. She's really nice, and she calls you Sweetie.*
>
> *Temperature down to 38.2 after the antibiotics. When samples return, they'll decide if they need to put...*

Mom is interrupted, probably by the nurse, Georgia, who comes in to take my vitals; however, James picks up the notebook and finishes her sentence for her.

> *...Tigger into a nursing home because he claims to be bouncing on his tail, but I saw him jumping instead in a game once.*

James can be a little nonsensical at times, but thank God we now know the ending to that sentence!

June 26, 2009

My stomach is doing better, so they start the feeding tube again slowly to see how it will go. Dr. Meadows explains to Mom how they'd be transitioning me out of my coma, slowly at first, over the weekend, with incremental decreases in medication to see at what dose I'll begin to wake up. Mom writes that the doctors warn her I'll likely wake up confused and scared, especially with the tubes down my throat. She should attempt to keep me as calm as possible while explaining the importance of keeping still. If I can't do this, they will have to keep me under sedation for longer. Dr. Meadows will be back on Monday to see how everything went.

James writes:

I went home yesterday to bring Lindor in to keep Littlefoot company because he was getting lonely. I also tried to see Kristy, but she was sleeping every time I went. And I went three different times. But I did give her Agent E, who is Agent D's partner, to keep her safe for you. Both Kristy and Hanna sent back a card for you and pictures.

Followed by Mom:

The pump on your lung tube machine is off. It's now draining by itself. That's one more thing! Wonderful. The doctor reduced your BP meds, which helped lower your HR, which was a bit high due to your fever. I'm told not to be too worried.

Physio said you have the same range of motion today as yesterday; you are no tighter. Your right lung is good, but your left lung is weaker. It should improve and get stronger once they take you off the respirator. When that time comes, they'll be able to do more exercises to help you cough on your own, which will help your lungs get stronger. Grammie returned to her brother's for the night, and James went to feed Littlefoot and Lindor. He will be back later.

10:00 pm. I'm still here. You are all ready for bed with a beautiful braid and surrounded by your teddies. You look very content. I'm not too worried about you. We will see you when you wake up and address any concerns after we have more information. They gave you more fluids tonight to help your temperature and heart rate. HR 112, BP not displayed, CPP 53-12.

11:30 pm. Night, Sweetie. I'll see you in the morning. I'm usually here at 5:30, but I'm staying in the hospital, so if you need me, the nurses can call me on my cell—James calculated that it would take me three minutes to get here! I guess I'll have to take big steps to match him.

June 27, 2009

It was a good night. The extra fluids helped balance out my heart rate and blood pressure. My lungs are doing better today, too. They're getting stronger from both healing and the daily physical therapy. I should be able to breathe on my own soon. Mom mentioned that I got a card today from fellow volunteers at the Canadian Red Cross office in Charlottetown. Mom and I have been volunteering to be part of the Disaster Management Team for PEI.

12:00 pm. The doctor was in. He's pleased with the levels. He reduced your sedation meds a bit more. We're still waiting on a consultation about removing your chest tube.

Around 2:00 pm, they took you off the sedation meds to see how long it would take for you to wake up, but then the doctor called around 3:30, saying they were putting you back on sedation until the morning since they couldn't remove your chest tube. You were trying really hard to wake up with your eyes twitching and moving, which was exciting, but tomorrow will be the day.

Mom.

June 28, 2009

Good morning, Sunshine. You had a great night. They're going to start reducing the medication that is helping you sleep. They need to confirm that your chest x-ray will be good for them to do this. Grammie, James, your dad and stepmom are all here. XO

3:00 pm. The doctor decided not to remove your chest tube today, and they will continue to monitor your responses. So excited when the nurse asked you to give her a thumbs up, and you actually did! I couldn't be happier.

Mom.

Mom works with clients with severe mental disabilities. I can only imagine how the worst-case scenario cannot get out of her head. But, of course, waiting an extra day to take me off my meds is just giving me more time to heal, and that must be why she is handling it so well.

8:00pm. You've had your bath and are ready for bed. All teddies are back on your bed for the night.

I was a big fan of stuffed animals when I was growing up, so Mom is making sure to nest me in them for comfort, as a mother would in her situation. James writes:

I am bored. Wake up already. I played The Sims 3 all day and am halfway to becoming an astronaut! I don't have many friends, but I'm working on it. By the way, it looks like you're being attacked by teddies all the time.

June 29, 2009

CT scan first thing, along with chest x-ray. Dr. Meadows was in to say the scan looked good and that he would take the probe out of your head, which he did. You are breathing independently, but now the hard work will be coughing and strengthening your lungs. Your respiratory doctor, Dr. Bray, was in and she said she's going to leave your chest tube in for one more day. Breathe deep. The time will come.

Mom.

Finally, they start taking me off my sedation and pain meds, even though the feeding tube is still down my throat. Dr. Meadows knows I won't take long to start waking up, so he is here to ask me some initial questions. He asks me to do some simple things, like open and close my eyes, and to squeeze his hand and let go. I pass most of the tests, which is great; this tells quite a bit about my cognitive state. Being able to not only hear him, but also to comprehend what he's saying, and then act accordingly within a reasonable time, is by itself a big map of directions my brain must navigate. Unfortunately, the left side of my body is still healing and cannot get fully tested just yet. Mom speaks to me when he leaves, knowing I can hear her.

"Hi Kamya, it's your mom," she says. "You were in a car accident in Charlottetown. You're now in Moncton, at the hospital here. You're probably sore and might feel a bit weird. Remember, it's important that you don't talk or move. You have a tube in your mouth right now, helping us get food into your stomach. Once you start eating for yourself, who knows, maybe we will have to sit you up like Littlefoot." At this, Mom giggles to herself, obviously joking. "You have a tube down your throat, so please don't try to talk—that will come. Until then, I don't know if you can remember this, but you learned some sign language a few years ago. You can move your right hand and use that to communicate with me for now. Do you understand what I am saying?" Mom holds her breath, desperate for me to communicate with her. Slowly, with all my might, I ball my right hand into a fist and lift it off the bed, making a soft thump noise as it comes back down. A lazy version of the sign for yes. Exhausted, I can hear my mom's excitement as she jumps up a little, eyes shining with tears. That's a sign her daughter knows. I feel glad I can give her that little bit of relief. My mind isn't ready to comprehend much more.

The room quickly becomes alert. "What?! What happened?!" asks the nurse, quickly scanning my body for any tubes or needles out of place or pried out.

"No, no, no." Mom reassures her. "I asked her a question and suggested she use sign language to communicate. And she just answered me!" The nurse's eyes widen and she swirls out of the room to get the doctor. Dr. Meadows enters the room quickly, curious about all the commotion.

"Ask her another question," he tells my mom.

"Kamya, do you have a dog named Rover?" She's starting simple. I focus on my hand, still balled into a fist, poke out the middle and index finger, lift them and tap the bed again. The sign for no, or a version of it anyway. Everyone gasps. The doctor just shakes his head and looks at Mom. "She's answered all our questions correctly so far, and now we've established a form of communication. She'll be just fine," he tells her and leaves the room.

I'm exhausted, and I rest back to sleep as I listen to the nurse ask Mom questions about whether I may have hearing problems. The truth is that when I was younger, Mom took a course in ASL to help her communicate with a new client at work, and she practised the basics with me. As a result, we often used simple signs, just for fun so we wouldn't forget what we learned.

After some rest, my physiotherapist (PT) enters the room to do breathing exercises and help me cough. It's terribly painful. It makes me want to go back to sleep, but everyone seems to think it's important. I feel the pressure to do my best, and my best isn't great. The PT finally leaves, and I get to rest my eyes. I don't think anyone understands just how exhausting this feels. Mom turns back to the notebook to communicate her excitement with me, while I close my eyes.

> *You're resting now, but later, they are going to try to get you to sit up in a chair to get you to cough more. You so amaze me. Brilliant.*

> *You just woke up and coughed, so I came to your bed. You were beating up Agent D in your right hand, but when I put my hand under yours, you signed L and O. I wasn't sure what the rest was going to be; you stopped there and drifted off again. But, just in case, I told you, "I love you too."*

> *Mom.*

Grammie picks up the notebook while I sleep:

KAMYA RILLING

I've been close by every day since your accident. You were a real trooper through all those tests the doctors and nurses gave you. Yesterday was Monday, and I told you yesterday that we will do something special when you get home. I thought you smiled, but I wasn't sure, so I said, "Kamya, did you just smile at me?" And you nodded your head a little to say yes. What a special day this is! You're awake now! You are a feisty one (we always knew that). Get well soon!! I love you lots.

Grammie.

Chapter Three: One Step at a Time

June 30, 2009

Now that the sedation meds have worn off and I'm officially awake, my first task is to strengthen my lungs. The physiotherapist and nurses work to sit me up so that I can cough and my lungs can get stronger.

> *James and I sat beside you. James is trying to finish the crossword puzzles I started but never finished. You are tired, and weak, but they are feeding you with a feeding tube, which should give you more energy.*
>
> *Mom.*

Even with the breathing tube out, I still prefer using Mom to help translate my simple signs, such as *yes, no, toilet, water,* or pointing directions. While everyone is still impressed that I can sign, they're confused about why I won't speak. Since I'm not speaking and resting most of the time, they still turn to the notebook to communicate with me. Dr. Meadows tells Mom that sometimes, if a patient is traumatized, they might be too afraid to talk or ask questions that they might not want the answers to. He suggested that she try to explain more about what happened to reassure me. Still, he will assign a speech therapist to visit and evaluate my ability to speak and swallow.

Dad, who hasn't written in the notebook yet, but who arrived the day after I did, adds an entry:

Kamya, you are looking much better every day and impressing me with your progress. Keep it up! I will be here for you. Your stepmom is here, too, but she stays out of the room so you can rest. There are enough people here as it is. I love you.

Dad.

Then Mom writes:

James went shopping for a new pair of sneakers for you now that you are awake and might start moving. He brought two pairs to choose from. He held up the two pairs, and you pointed to the ones with the light green stripes. But they were too big when we tried them on, so back to the store James went.

Mom.

July 1, 2009

Busy day. Dr. Meadows discharged you from the ICU (intensive care unit), which was terrific. But really, you just got moved nearby. Your new room is smaller and has a different wall space, so I just put a few cards up on the wall.

I get my chest and feeding tubes out and start drinking out of a straw. Swallowing takes effort, though. I have to focus more on this than I've ever done in my life. Mom tells me she's keeping track of what I'm eating. I'm glad I don't have to do that.

You were off to sleep at 10:30, so now I'm off to bed.

I think it's funny how she still feels the need to write that down for me. I can see though, that details written in the notebook could be helpful to me in the future, when I'm ready to read it.

July 2, 2009

The respirator aid is back, and she gave me another disgusting oral rinse to help prevent infections. They're still giving me my asthma medication, I think, so an oral flush every now and then is to prevent thrush from developing. My occupational therapist and physiotherapist work together to get me out of bed and sitting up in a chair for the first time since I arrived.

Your dad brought you some new clothes, including boxers, to choose from. You had a busy day and are tired, so we will wait to show you later to see if you like them. James will get you some stuff at home too. The unit doctor, Dr. Parker, called to say he was happy with the results of your CT scan. Everything is healing great. He has asked for more physio on your chest/lungs to help heal your punctured lung faster.

You have your new sneakers James picked out, and they fit perfectly. We are still waiting to hear how the x-ray on your collarbone went.

July 3, 2009

Now that James got me the sneakers I wanted, I'm taken to the gym in physio to see if I can try standing. Unfortunately, I've lost weight, my muscles feel weak, and I can't hold myself up without help. I don't know how much of it is from being in bed for over a week or from my sad left side. Both the physiotherapist and Mom are trying to convince me to try standing up. My legs feel like a deflated cartoon. *Maybe this is too soon*, I think, feeling disheartened and not at all confident in myself.

Mom catches James in the hallway to help. He's always been the most athletic of the family and knows more about the human body's capability than I think I'll ever know. I know he wouldn't expect me to be the weakling, scaredy pants I'm being now. He knows better than that, and I won't be able to get away with it. All he does is give me this look. This, *Get the fuck up,* look. This, *I don't give a shit what you're feeling, I've been sitting in this hospital for over a week waiting for this,* kind of look.

"Come on Kamya, you can do this. Just follow me," he says.

I sigh and let the physiotherapist help me onto my feet. It feels good, not as painful as I expected, especially considering all my internal injuries. I wince only a little but feel secure with James in front of me.

I prove to him that I can take a couple of tiny steps. Walking for the first time, I feel like a robot. My joints are stiff, mechanical as I sway to lift my leg and take that extra step and land it while everyone holds onto me so I don't fall. The walking bars help, they guide me forward, but it's slow-going with a lot of resistance. I'm too focused to panic, to even notice how slowly I'm going; I'm not looking at anything but my legs and concentrating so hard on dragging them forward an inch at a time. When I finally reach the end of the exercise, I look up and it looks like I haven't moved. I feel done, though. This will have to be enough.

They let me sit back in my chair and we go to my room so I can rest for the remainder of the day.

July 4, 2009

About a week and a half after my accident, and I now have no feeding tube. I will have to learn how to swallow food again. Hospital food may not be the most appetizing, but it's the first food I've tasted in a while so it's actually pretty good. What would be great, though, is some of that lobster that Aunt Izzy promised. We're still in lobster season, right?

Mom continues in my notebook still.

Sat! You sat up in a chair for a couple of hours, and we went for a walk. It was nice to get out of your room! Feeding tube out. Nose is itchy as hell, and it's a new day!

July 5, 2009

You were wide awake today and full of questions. We signed yes and no as well as spelling out with letters, and communicated about how you were feeling and how hard you'll work to improve. You got up into a shower chair, and I helped you shower, and yes, you got me wet. Then, you got dressed, and out of the hospital pyjamas. We returned to the room to find James, Dad, and your stepmom. You saw the pizza box on the table, pointed to it and then yourself, and smiled. Of course, I wasn't sure if you could eat it yet, but I gave you a small piece of cheese to try. You didn't handle it as well as you should have so I don't think you're ready to eat and swallow a piece of pizza, but as soon as you can I will get it delivered right to your room.

Now, my determined young lady, your main objective today was to convince everyone to move you from the wheelchair to the soft recliner chair in the waiting room. After you got many 'no's, you won. I showed James and Dad how to move you, and you lounged back and stretched and were very content.

Back home to PEI soon, I promise.

Chapter Four: Back Home

We're returning to the Island, riding first class. An ambulance is better than the backseat of a car, right? Plenty of room to stretch and lounge. Looking out the back window, I see the verdant forests of New Brunswick streaming by beside the highway. I wonder what the other drivers on the highway think this ambulance is for. Do they know I'm back here? Do they understand the significance of me going across the bridge today? Of course not. Everybody is out there, living their own lives. I may have been asleep most of the time since my accident, but I know I miss home. There's nowhere else I would rather spend my time healing. I look at Mom beside me, hoping she feels the same relief. She looks just as exhausted as I am.

"We're going onto the bridge soon, Kamya!" Mom says.

I close my eyes again. Getting onto the bridge is always a milestone when going to PEI. One of the longest bridges in the world that crosses cold open water, the Confederation Bridge takes so long to pass over that you can forget you're on a bridge. It's one of those facts about PEI I think is underappreciated. There's a lot more to us than pretty views and being polite if we're important enough for a bridge like this to be here. I look out the window and see familiar grey cement walls that line the bridge, and over them, a glimpse of clear blue water that glimmers like sapphire. Bright as a blue sky on a summer's day. Brighter, actually. The line that separates the blue of the sky and the blue of an ocean is visible because the water has a lot more to it; something is unique in the water that the sky will never have. I brace for the bump under the tires, and we are here, back on solid ground again.

"Soon, we'll be in your room and getting it all set up for you!" Mom says with a big smile; it turns out she is feeling that same optimistic relief now that we're going home. It feels like a move forward—closer to getting better and getting my life back, no longer sitting stagnant in a hospital bed in an unfamiliar environment. Charlottetown is closer to home. The comfort of this lets me fall back asleep.

Arriving at the Queen Elizabeth Hospital in Charlottetown, I breathe in the Island air. I barely get a chance to enjoy the fresh air before they place me in a wheelchair and send me to my new room. Once there, I point to the colourful cards Mom put on the table beside my bed and point to the wall. I imagine we're staying here a while and I'm anxious to make this feel as homey as possible.

"You want me to put your cards up? But we might still be transferred to a better room. We don't know how long we will be in this one," Mom says.

I point and then point again. I'm not sitting in a drab, white room while trying to find encouragement. I need some colour. She orders James to put up a couple of cards, but just enough to make me happy. I rest in my bed and get ready to meet my new team of caretakers.

The first person I meet is my new physiotherapist, Tassa. I'm expecting to spend a lot of time there learning how to walk again and likely discovering some other physical abilities I may need improvement on. She first meets me in my room to explain the work she expects of me while I'm here. It's nice that she's talking to me directly about the physical work I will be doing. It makes it more real, like I'll have to do this work and it's not just Mom who needs to lead me.

Soon, fatigue washes over me with the thought of all the work ahead. Can I even walk at all? My legs feel weak right now. I can barely inch my good side into a more comfortable position, and my left isn't budging. I express my concerns to Mom, speaking in a broken, low, airy voice, while trying to compensate with gestures using my right hand. I'm just a bit taken over by my reality and wondering about my walking abilities. She gives me a look.

"Kamya, you already went walking back in Moncton. James and I were there, in the gym. You took three steps! They may have been small, but you definitely walked!"

I'm shocked to hear this. *Seriously?* I try to give her a strange look. I think I would have remembered something as significant as that. There's no way, but, hey, if she says I can walk, I must be able to walk. It comforts me a little, even if it's a white lie.

Next up is my occupational therapist (OT). I have no idea what work I'll be doing with her, but her name is Edith. Apparently, I had an OT in Moncton too. Another thing I don't remember. Not remembering isn't that big a deal to me. I understand that my brain has been affected—I can feel it in my muddy thoughts and constant fatigue. What I don't know is when I can expect to start retaining information again, like a normal person. Until then, I have no choice but to depend on others. Mom says that back in Moncton, my OT helped work out some of my muscles the same way my physiotherapist did, but it might be different here. An OT is supposed to help me get back to living my normal life, doing everyday things that people normally do with no trouble. She can help me cook, study for school, drive a car, etc. Unfortunately, I won't find out today. During my visit with Edith we stay in my room and exchange pleasantries and updates. I'm grateful because her visit has exhausted me, and I've already fallen asleep before she leaves.

When I wake up, Mom is packing up my special shampoos. We're moving to the new room they promised us—just when I was starting to feel comfortable. I get wheeled into this new room with a noticeable size difference. With a single bed in the middle, I see a decent-sized window where I can see the innocent light-blue sky. It's more of a cloudy white, but my imagination takes hold. I can't say it's a reflection of my current optimism; to be honest, I can't say I'm feeling either pessimistic or optimistic right now. I'm only focused on the work ahead. Imagining a calming blue sky though, is making me feel just a little bit better. Now that we're in a room Mom's happy about, I don't have to argue with her to put my cards up on the wall.

"What makes this room special is that it's closer to the nurses' desk so that if I'm not here, all you have to do is press this button, and someone will be here in seconds," Mom says as she finishes putting up my cards on the wall and comes to sit beside the bed.

She motions to a small white rod with a red button on its head attached to my bed. I mumble a joke to Mom, asking when she is not here. She takes it seriously and starts explaining her work schedule to me, explaining when she will be here to accompany me, so I don't ever have to feel alone. I'm getting tired again after simply listening to her. I rarely go away from my bed anyway, especially not by myself. Even though Mom has assured me I can walk, no one trusts me to move an inch away from the middle of the bed. I feel glued in place, unable to move on my own. I'm peeled from the wheelchair and stuck in the bed until someone can help me get up again.

My dad walks into my room and looks around with his eyebrows dramatically raised, and makes a sweet comment about how nice it is and how comfortable I look in my hospital bed. I bet I look comfortable—it's not like I can move anyway. He hugs and kisses me goodbye before returning home to work in the States. Mom works here in Charlottetown, so it's easier for her to stay. I think James is remaining nearby, too. *I mean, where else would he go?* I think as a joke to myself, but in reality I know he's busy with university courses and a summer job. When he visits, James spends most of his time pushing me back and forth to my appointments in my wheelchair. He makes a game of it. It's hard to push a wheelchair, though, you know that? He crashed me into the wall a few times, and people just stared at us! He pretends he's doing it on purpose. Honestly, it gives me more laughs than I've had in a long time—more than I remember, that is.

I'm starting speech therapy. I still can't speak above a small whisper, and the doctors think I may need help learning to use my voice again. This therapist's name is Carlton—"Like in *Fresh Prince*," Mom explains. I miss watching that show after school. Unfortunately, I can't watch any TV in my room because I'm told it would be too much stimulation for my healing brain. So I'm left to just imagine Carlton on TV, doing his Carlton dance with Will Smith beside him joining along. This makes me smile—Will Smith was my favourite growing up.

Mom mistakes my smile as a sign of laughter over the cue cards given to us with pictures of facial expressions to practise. The downside of mainly being mute, I guess. I honestly don't have the energy to correct her. In my mind, I don't care what I look like, I only want to learn how to communicate with words again. It's just as much work to me as the work I do in physio. They may be funny faces to her, but to me they are work. After showing me how to mouth a few vowel sounds, Carlton notices how tired I am and leaves.

Dr. Bryan, the unit doctor, comes to my room in the mornings for regular check-ups and to see how I'm doing with my therapy. I've been doing at least two types of treatment a day since I got here. I don't know how long I've been here—a week, maybe two? The days are all blurring together. Time isn't a concept I can fully grasp right now. He leaves my room satisfied with my progress, and I lie in bed with my eyes closed when suddenly, a thought pops up in my head.

My eyes crunch, then widen, and I see Mom sitting beside me. I don't understand. Where's Dad? Why hasn't he even come to visit me yet? And Kristy, Hanna, my aunts Izzy and Amelia, or any other friends or family? None of them have even asked about me since I arrived on the Island. Mom is looking at me, confused. I try my best to communicate this through barely audible whispers and hand gestures without panicking. I'm aggressively signing "father," "grandmother," "family," but forgetting the sign for "friends."

I wonder if I'm not communicating right, but of course, Mom understands what I'm asking. She explains that everyone, all of them, have been in to see me very recently. Kristy and Hannah are both okay and safe at home. Dad was here just a few days ago, but he had to say goodbye to go back to the States for work. *Wow. What? No. Okay.* I give her a blank stare for as long as I can muster, before all my strength and ambition leave me and I begin nodding off again. I hope my look got it across to her that I don't remember any of that. I have no idea what she's talking about.

The following day, Mom is at my bedside while I try to finish my breakfast of simple foods that require minimal chewing. I still need to be monitored while I eat—*which is fun,* I think sarcastically to myself. I look at her with that same blank stare I gave her last night, trying to communicate with my mind, but feeling like nothing is getting through. I can't remember how that conversation ended. Did it have an ending? Why can't I remember things? How bad, exactly, is this brain injury?

On his morning rounds, Dr. Bryan comes into the room with a smile. Mom immediately brings up our conversation from last night.

"A brain injury is one of the most complicated injuries," he starts. "The exhaustion can affect her more than expected. Because of her injury, her brain won't work like a normal brain. Even simple things can take longer and use more energy." He looks towards me now. "In time, the brain will make new neural connections to replace the ones you've lost." Mom sits on the end of the bed, calculating my new reality just as I'm trying to.

"However," Dr. Bryan continues, "this process of creating new passageways can greatly tax the brain, making you more tired. The more tired you are, the harder it will be for your brain to function. We won't know the total outcome of the brain injury until enough time passes. Focusing so much on her therapy could be putting strain on her short-term memory, causing things to not register like they normally would. It's frustrating, but we'll have to wait and see."

Wait?! Mom looks calm and collected, so maybe this is just a reality that I've yet to process. He said I may take more time to process things, so I will give myself time. Focus on my therapies. If I don't know if I should panic yet, then why bother panicking?

Back from physio and OT, I've already forgotten about the trouble I was having with my memory. Both are strenuous, but the exercises I do in OT make me feel stupid. Now that my collarbone has almost healed, Edith gives me the simplest things to do with my left hand. She asks me to pick up a button and move it to the other side of the table. It's arduous work. My hand doesn't want to listen, and my shoulder gets in the way somehow, and Edith growls whenever I move my feet with the rest of my body, as if I can help it. With time, I hope it'll get better. At least she tells me I am doing better than yesterday, but I doubt it. The frustration I feel takes my mind away from optimism, and it only makes me feel anger.

I am back in bed now, exhausted. James brings out my CD player and suggests we play some of the music I had in Moncton. My memories of the Moncton stay are so confusing. I can't trust any of them. They aren't really there, and when I think they are I don't know if they're real. Mostly, I rely on the short stories mom has shared with me more recently about my time in Moncton and everything else since my accident. Those are helping, at least.

"There's a book fair upstairs in the lobby today. You love books," Mom says one morning. "Maybe you and James can go up there to browse? We could buy any book you want, especially if it gets you reading. It could keep you busy while you're sitting here in bed." She says this as if I'm not always sleeping.

I agree, remembering my love of books, too, although none really come to mind at this moment. James and I get set up to head upstairs.

James plants my wheelchair in front of a selection of books and leaves me so he can explore for himself. Since arriving at QEH, I've learned to navigate the wheelchair independently—something I learned in OT. I push forward with my right hand and steer with my right foot. OT, as it turns out, is not only about getting back to normal but also about learning how to use my strengths.

I wave to get James' attention— he's already found an old *Ghostbusters* comic to read. After getting his attention, I point toward the larger, hardcover nonfiction books on the table a few feet away. James pushes me over and gets distracted by something on the next table. I don't know why he didn't just start here first; this is more his speed. Various science books are mixed in with a couple of thick autobiographies. I struggle to pick up a book with my one working hand. My left arm is still in a cast from the broken collarbone—*clavicle*, I correct myself; I want to use the proper names. This book has a transparent image of a human body on the front cover. Its title, *The Human Body*, is written across an image of a torso, right below the clavicle. I quickly look around to see if there might be any books on the brain, but I can't find any. I motion to James and whisper (mostly clearly now) to him to look for me, but he comes up empty-handed. This will have to do. James buys it for me and we head back to the room.

Satisfied with my find, I open it as soon as I'm comfortably back in bed. Mom laughs at me and says I had to choose the biggest book at the fair. In her defence, it's big and awkward for my lap, but in my defence, I'm just about sick and tired of none of this making any sense to me, so I'm trying! It's not long before my grip on the book loosens, and James takes it away from me before it falls to the floor. Not much of a nap, though, before lunch is placed before me. It's that nasty Jell-O again—"booster" as Mom calls it. Supposedly, it has all the nutrients I need to help me recover faster.

Okay, but you will feed me that lobster at some point, right? I think, as I reluctantly pick up the spoon while Mom opens the package for me. My eyes start to water with the thought of its metallic flavour in my mouth, and I can feel my mouth slowly forming a look of disgust; not so much, I hope, that anyone can see it. Truthfully, I have been feeling stronger lately. I'd have to be strong to lift my new book with only one hand. I take the spoon and feed myself a small spoonful of the jelly. The first bite is always the worst until I get used to its flavour. I'm not so good at hiding my disgust this time, and Mom sees it. She looks at me as if *I'm* the one being difficult.

"What are you doing, making that face?" she asks, "It's yummy Jell-O! It smells so delicious! I think you should eat something healthier, but the nurses say it's the best thing for you. Apparently, it has a bunch of vitamins and good stuff mixed into it somehow."

I look down and grimace. This might be the best thing for my facial exercises. *I think I'd rather get my vitamins and nutrients the old fashioned way,* I think to myself, even with how tiring it is to focus and chew.

Unfortunately, my communication skills won't allow me to put that into a sentence. Setting the spoon down between each bite, I hope for it to magically disappear. James walks in and notices me being 'difficult.' My twenty-year-old big brother takes the Jello-O from me, smells it, and goes on about how delicious it smells. I know he's full of it—he's not fooling anyone. He takes a big bite with my spoon before I can get his attention and tell him not to. A genuine look of disgust spreads over his face. I burst out in silent laughter. He looks at Mom and tells her that I must no longer eat this "disgusting gross Jell-O wannabe," and then he leaves to look for something better for me, although I know he's unlikely to come up with anything. I take a big sigh and relax in my seat. Thank God for James. Mom would never have tried that.

The next morning, Mom comes in with a massive container of protein powder that James picked out. She takes an old plastic shaker from home out of her purse, pauses, and puts both on the bedside table before leaving the room, saying she'll be back. I reach for the table conveniently placed on my right side and pull it closer, examining the tub of protein powder. It has a picture of vanilla ice cream on it and looks delicious. Mom returns with some chocolate milk in hand and scoops out some powder to add to the milk in the shaker. I watch her shake it and put it in a paper cup.

"It's just protein powder usually used by people who want to get fit, and I guess you're trying to get fit, aren't you? I'm not sure what this will taste like. James picked it out for you last night and gave me instructions. The nurses had no white milk, so I hope chocolate will be okay."

Chocolate milk does sound good. I take a sip, my eyes widen, my heart jumps, and I immediately bring the cup back to my mouth. It's as if I haven't consumed anything in the last month. I drink only one gulp before Mom takes it away, growling about how I could have choked by drinking too fast. I don't care. I can feel my skin buzzing. It's the most alive I've felt in a long time. I looked at her solemnly. She's too protective, but she really doesn't need to worry. I've been practising swallowing enough to control some thick chocolate milk.

Visitors come on the weekends with gifts for my room, and questions to help spark my memory. My bosses from The Toy Factory come to see me. They ask me questions, and I answer most of them correctly. They don't stay long, though. I can't take too much stimulation yet and having too many visitors in my room at once is a lot. Mom's always protecting me from too much stimulation.

Before long, I'm back to my hard work and therapy. I have no idea how long it's been since the accident. This is my life now, whether I want it or not. I asked for the best treatment possible and now Mom says she won't let me give up. Sitting on a bed in physio, waiting for Tassa to finish with her last patient, some familiar patients come and go. A middle-aged couple settles on the bed beside mine, and I smile at them. They're often in the gym at the same time as me. I've seen Mom talking to the wife while her husband gets treated by the physiotherapist. From what she tells me, he was in an accident where two vehicles crushed him—both his legs were destroyed, and his face and body showed signs of the trauma, too. He's also been working hard in physio every day. Even though I certainly wish that hadn't happened to him, it's nice to see that I'm not alone. It feels like we're best friends, even without knowing or speaking to each other. I heard him speak once, but only a little, and it sounded hoarse and painful. Other than that, he's usually as silent as I am. Both of us lie on our beds, close enough that we can turn our heads and see each other. He smiles at me and speaks with his warm eyes, and I smile back. I wish I could get to know him better, but Tassa interrupts our silent conversation to tell me to start doing my leg exercises, where I lift my leg, count to three, drop it, and lift it again. I give him a look that says "Back to it," and his response is one of sincere understanding. It's a tough exercise, even for my right side, but Tassa says I have to do the exercises on both, even if my left needs the most work.

"We must focus on both sides to keep symmetry as much as possible. That's our goal," she says.

Back down in my unit, I have enough energy after a quick nap to let James help guide me while walking in the hall. My one physio appointment a day makes progress feel slow. I often walk down the hallway, towards the entry doors and back, wearing a big blue belt around my waist with someone gripping its side to ensure I don't fall. I prefer walking with James in these situations. It feels a lot safer than when he pushes my wheelchair. Plus, when Mom holds my belt, she always keep a death grip to hold me up. I hold myself up just fine. The strap is there just in case I suddenly can't.

Almost to the door, with one hand on the hall railing, I focus on each motion my legs make, my weight distribution on the floor and the other leg free in the air. Stop and repeat on the other side. I focus away from every thought to concentrate fully, not taking big steps. I don't have enough trust in myself to freefall into the next step as much as I now notice people do without thinking. The amount of power that people have and take for granted is astonishing. Without really thinking about it, they can lift their legs and fall into the next step without concentration! And unquestioningly trust that the floor will catch them! It blows my mind. Who knew that's all walking was? At the entry doors, an old teacher of mine arrives to visit me with a smile and widened eyes. I never would have expected to see him here, and he never would have expected me to greet him at the doors.

I slowly start to feel proud of myself. I guess it's impressive: waking up from a coma with a brain injury and instantly being able to communicate using sign language. I answer a lot of probing memory questions correctly when people come to visit me, including how I know them, how we met, simple trivia questions on details I might have known from before my brain injury, like knowledge of books or school. I even get the math questions right. I get it, it's amazing—but it doesn't feel amazing.

The sign language I know is simple: *yes, no, hello, goodbye*. I know the alphabet if I sit and think about it for long enough, and I can do random essential words like *toilet, eat,* and *go* but I still need Mom's help reminding me what certain words are. I can't communicate complete sentences to explain myself to people, and my whispering is no better.

I feel lost most of the time. I take a step, and it's miraculous. A step. A freaking step. I sigh and think, *I should stop thinking so negatively or it'll become a habit.* A single step is the most amazing thing ever. Most people don't realize the concentration it takes. Most people walk around everywhere, every day, quickly getting from point A to point B, without ever realizing how miraculous their bodies are. Their brains are miraculous for knowing how to move without much thought. Brains are amazing. I can't always be on edge about how my brain injury will turn out. I want to have fun, too.

The next couple of weeks of daily therapy feel like forever. Struggling to move like a normal human being is challenging. Some days are more manageable—I stretch my legs, do simple exercises, stand up, take a few steps, and see progress. Other times, I see no progress or feel like I'm falling behind. Moving on to a new physiotherapist, I'll now work with Jesse. She has experience working with stroke patients and is excited to start working with me. Right off the bat, we get along. She has such a bubbly personality and loves to chat. Her cheerful blonde perm is a nice distraction at times. We talk as we work, making the time go by faster. From what I can tell, I can do as much work as I want to improve, but I'll never be fully back to normal. I've been reminded many times to prepare for a whole new way of life. I don't believe I'll ever be considered "normal" again. Not that I remember what normal was like anyway.

Walking with Jesse at my side and taking my steps, my left leg decides not to listen. I trip over it, catch myself with my right, and wait for Jesse to ask if I'm okay. Of course I am, physically, but mentally it puts me down. *Why can't my leg just listen to me and lift the goddamn foot?!* Other people don't have to deal with this problem. The helplessness, the fear, and the feeling that I'm a waste of space all put pressure on my mind. My head starts to hurt a little. I sigh and tear up, looking at Jesse as she speaks encouraging words.

"It's okay, Kamya. Just start again. With practice, your body will start to get used to the new commands your brain is sending, and you just wait; you'll be able to do the full ten steps towards me without tripping once!" Repeating her advice to myself, I sigh and start over. It's certainly not perfect, but it'll do for now.

"You're still dragging your left foot a lot. Can you do something for me? Try to lift your toes while keeping your heel on the ground. Like this," she says as she demonstrates.

I look down and tilt my head, uncertain and hesitant.

"Start with your right. Yes, that's it! It's not great, but you can certainly do it! Now, try your left."

I do the same to my left, but nothing happens. This foot stays on the ground, and I swear I'm putting more effort in than I did with my right. The foot should have shot up by now, but it won't listen to me, and it won't move. I look at Jesse, defeated. *This is my problem, isn't it? This is why I'm so unsteady.* She lets me sit on the bed just as my friend and his wife get up to leave. I feel beaten, but I'm certainly not one to crush the hopes and encouragement of others around me. I can't let them know how frustrated I am. I just can't.

"Are you still wearing that big boot that helps stretch your calf muscle while you sleep or lie down?"

I nod. I hate that thing so much. Mom calls it my transformer boot. I call it the thing that doesn't help me sleep or be comfortable.

"Hmm... Hold on."

She leaves me for a few minutes, my feet dangling off the bed. Then, finally, she comes back with a small piece of fabric that looks like upholstery.

"Here, give me your left shoe. This is a sturdy material so that you can walk on it, but it's also workable, so we can ensure it's the right size and shape for you. By using this extra little lift, it encourages your heel to hit the ground before your toes, allowing your foot to be in proper walking formation."

She puts it in the heel of my shoe, gets me to stand up, examines my foot, takes the shoe off, leaves again briefly with the lift material, and comes to put it back in my shoe again. I sit there like a rag doll, waiting for permission to leave. The second time she examines my foot, she tells me to get up and take a few steps, holding her hands. I do, and it's noticeably easier.

She nods when she sees I'm having an easier time. "You'll have to wear this lift in your shoe while walking until your calf muscles loosen up. Right now, it looks like you're walking on your toes, and this is because the muscles in your calves are so tight from lying in your hospital bed so much, which isn't good, but it's something we can work on slowly over time."

Hey, walking is walking, right? It shouldn't be that big a deal if I'm hitting the ground toes first instead of the heel, but I guess it looks funny. Mom says I should strive to look normal, or else I can expect people to constantly ask me what's wrong or if I'm okay, which I know will be annoying. She might just be using this as encouragement, though.

In my room, Mom reminds me that Kristy's visiting today and begins listing things we could do together. It's been forever since I've been able to hang out with a friend. I don't remember anything from the day of the accident we were in together. I'm sure she's worried about me, but this is life. Bad things happen. You just have to pick up the pieces you have left and make the most of it.

I'm excited to see her. She's one of those people I can fully be myself around. Knowing I won't have to hide anything from her is a relief. I won't have to be the polite young woman who just does what she's told. We spend the day together doing the things on my list, including visiting the gift shop, colouring in my colouring book, shaving my legs, and having dinner together.

After dinner I want to cry when I remember she's leaving soon and I'll be going back to my life simply as a patient, but I can't ruin it, so I hold it in. Really, what's there to cry about? I'll have nothing to do but rest in bed and relax once she leaves. I'll probably forget I was even close to crying when morning comes and I'm back in therapy.

* * *

I wake up in my hospital bed and stretch, bracing myself to re-enter the never-ending loop of therapies and memory games. Memories of my life growing up become clearer and clearer. I remember my old school. I vaguely remember the view from our front porch. I also remember some small things that Mom never knew about. Like the imaginary friend I used to play with outside when I was younger or certain games I played with the neighbour's kids.

Things like that I remember: the ordinary, simple, and significant.

My favourite food was Grampie's picnic ham and scalloped potatoes. I salivate when I think of it. I wonder if it would still be my favourite food now. Supposedly, a change in the palate can happen after a brain injury; isn't that scary? Imagine not being able to enjoy one of life's greatest pleasures: the taste food. There are very few things I don't remember; most of them have to do with the day or week of the accident. It can be hard to know what's considered significant and what isn't. Life is so strange.

I sit patiently and wait for Mom. She's promised a special breakfast this morning. My favourite breakfast is Mom's eggs benedict, but I'm going to miss that this year. Today's my seventeenth birthday, but I'm spending the day in the hospital. What would a typical seventeen-year-old be doing for their birthday? I don't think seventeen is an important year socially, not like a sweet sixteen at least, so maybe it's not so bad that I'm in the hospital for it. I probably would've spent my birthday at home otherwise.

Finally, Mom enters my room with a breakfast tray in hand. She has a large, proud smile as she sets it before me on my little table.

"Good morning, Birthday Girl! I've got your special birthday breakfast right here!" She unveils the tray to expose a typical scrambled eggs hospital breakfast but with hollandaise sauce over the eggs. My eyes widen. It's not quite her benedict but at least it has the hollandaise, which is the best part. God bless her.

"I don't know how it will taste on scrambled eggs. I made the sauce at home, brought some in, heated it, and stole your tray from the cart to add it. I hope it will do. James and I had ours on poached eggs this morning."

To savour every bite, I eat it slowly, enjoying it. She will growl at me if I start eating too fast anyway.

"You're eating it so slowly. Don't you like it?"

Oh my God. Will nothing make her happy? I eat fast, and she lectures me; I eat slow, and she thinks I don't like the food. I carefully pause from eating, making sure there's no food left in my mouth that I can choke on before I answer.

"Yes, I'm enjoying it! I'm just being careful, so you don't bother me about eating too fast. Although what was the point since you're bothering me anyway because I'm eating too slow." It's a lot of words, so I'm not sure if she caught all of it, but my patience only stretches so far and my food is getting cold.

She replies, "Well, eat up because we need to make it to physio this morning!"

Make it to physio. Of course. Any hopes for a lazy, relaxing birthday are squashed. It would be nice to take a break from reality for a bit, but therapy waits for no one. I can't ask for a day off just because it's my birthday. I hope we can make it fun and not too difficult, but that isn't my decision.

The couple next to us in the gym wish me a happy birthday. Mom joins me for my appointments, spending all the time she can.

"Today is your birthday?!" Jesse exclaims. "How old are you turning?" I whisper that I'm seventeen, but the gym is too noisy for her to hear me, so I sit on the bed like a child while my mommy tells her how old I am. I certainly don't feel seventeen.

"Seventeen?! Wow. This is good timing, actually. Your doctor just told me he hopes to let you go home soon on a weekend pass. So it's my job to ensure you're ready for your journey!" *A weekend pass. A weekend pass?! Do I get to go home?!*

Mom sees the look on my face and explains. "A weekend pass is when you get to go home for just the weekend, but then you'll have to come back here on Monday morning for your normal appointments."

She wants to make sure I don't get too excited, or think I might finally be going home.

This is the best birthday present I could ask for right now, the promise to visit home and see my dogs. What else would I want? A bike?

Jesse explains that to start, we have to ensure I can get in and out of a car. Now it makes sense that they have a random old car inside the gym. That's practical I suppose. We'll also have to practise walking with my cane and having nobody at my side so I won't have to rely on my wheelchair, and so I can visit the washroom if no one's nearby.

"Oh, I will be by her side. Don't you worry about that. She won't be walking to the bathroom alone." Mom seems nervous, but I'll show her I can do it. I'll make sure that I can. It's a four-pronged cane, so it's sturdier than most hands that have helped me walk.

"No." Jesse looks at her. "It's one of the mandatory requirements Kamya needs to be able to fulfill before I can safely release her to go home for a visit." She says it strictly, almost lecturing Mom for being too protective. Good, I could use a little freedom. I can't learn how to walk alone if someone is holding me back. Mom has been a lot of help, but I'm starting to worry that maybe she's becoming overbearing. While I appreciate her urge to protect me, it is she, after all, who always tells me not to let anyone hold me back.

"I know," Mom says, "but we have stairs right near the bathroom, and I'm not sure if I'd feel comfortable having her walk past them on her own. Not just yet, anyway."

"Oh, you have stairs. I was going to ask you about that. If you have stairs, we should also practice climbing stairs."

"Our living space is upstairs on the same floor, but we have a basement. The basement is where the kids watch TV and hang out with friends, but I'll see if I can move the couch and TV upstairs before she comes home."

"That would be a good idea. Not that you'll be watching much TV, Kamya, but then you could have the couch to sit on if you need it," Jesse says. "That would mean we'll only have to try the stairs a little and make sure she could do them if needed." She looks at me with a confident smile.

I just sit there, keeping track of their conversation while they discuss plans for me in the coming days. I don't mind it, as long as I get to visit home. I no longer feel like a child when thinking about all the work and concentration coming my way. I just have to learn how to get in and out of a car properly, walk alone with a cane, and climb stairs. At least with stairs there's a railing I can hold onto. I watch Jesse and Mom as they size the mock stairs they have in the gym and compare them to the stairs we have at home. I don't know what's taking them so long. I can see from where I'm sitting that those stairs are perfect.

Back in my room, I'm happy to only have one appointment today. While I'm dreaming about returning home, Mom tells me she's put together another special meal for my birthday supper. She asked for my tray to include ham and scalloped potatoes. Those aren't on the standard menu, so the kitchen staff must have gone out of their way to make it for me.

It's unbelievable what people will do to make a complete stranger happy on her birthday. People are wonderful. As I close my eyes and slowly drift off, I feel pretty happy about my seventeenth birthday. Sure, it wasn't the usual fun birthday bash of a teenager, but I enjoyed it.

Over the next few days, I'm busy getting ready for my weekend pass. After weeks of being held in place, my left arm is finally out of the sling, but it keeps wanting to return to that bent position. As a result, I am constantly getting growled at to move my arm to my side, where it naturally *should* be.

By the time I'm supposed to go home for the weekend, I am a

master of the stairs—I can climb them with no help whatsoever, but my hand rests on the railing constantly, just in case. I have figured out the cane like a pro—the four-prongs make me feel secure, and I can walk a distance long enough to get to the bathroom down the hall at home. I wonder if Mom will at least let me try doing that walk alone. I would at least like to try it, if just to learn what I need to work on. Getting in and out of the car is proving to be the most difficult—go figure. I'm a far cry from being able to drive a car or get my license, that's for sure. The problem is that I'm focusing so much on my damn shoulder that I forget to concentrate on my legs and feet. I have to really focus to ensure my left shoulder is up high and at the correct angle to climb in safely. I feel like my whole body is a mess. Jesse helps me refocus my concentration, though. After only a couple of days, I pass the exam to be able to get in and out safely, and we are on to the next batch of challenges.

Chapter Five: The Next Step

The unit doctor wishes me good luck, tells Mom to call if there are any slips or falls, and tells me to enjoy my time out of the hospital. As Mom pushes me out of the hospital doors in a borrowed wheelchair, my eyes water. Proudly, I show Mom I have no problem getting into the car without help, and we start the 30-minute journey home with the windows down, the warm summer air flowing in to freshen my face.

Mom likes to listen to CDs in the car. I forgot she likes to do that. For today's ride, she has one of my favourite of her CDs, *Songs from the Heart* by Celtic Woman. I've spent many road trips with her, listening to the lyrics of these songs. Their song "Fields of Gold" is my favourite. It speaks of a woman with long hair in a golden field with her love. It hits home and reminds me of the soy fields growing around our house. Not that I would be running through one of these fields with a handsome man, but it's a beautiful image. I tell Mom to put that one on.

"Really? Is that one your favourite? I thought it was 'Galway Bay.'"

"I get why you would think that because we listen to it often, and I know all the words, but no. 'Galway Bay' is Lindor's favourite." I tell her about the times we took my dog Lindor to the vet, and I sang the song to him, so he'd stay calm in the car. Delighted to hear myself quietly speak a complete sentence, I look at Mom, and she doesn't even ask me to repeat it. It turns out that away from all the hospital noises and people, she can finally hear me! I start to cry, trying my best to hide it from Mom. *I'm going home on a weekend pass!*

She looks over and sees me crying. *Please don't make a big deal out of this.* But she doesn't. She ignores the tears rolling down my cheeks and me pulling up the hem of my shirt to wipe them away. I don't want to miss this. The look of the outside. The sun. The sky. The beautiful blue sky I imagined I saw on the ambulance ride home.

"It's so beautiful out," I whisper in my small, tired voice.

"What?" Mom asks loudly. She turns the music down so she can hear me.

"It's a nice day," I repeat, not the exact words, I know. But after a while, you get sick and tired of repeating yourself. Rephrasing seems to be the trick to get people to say "What?" only once.

I don't wait for her reply. Instead, I reach for the volume to turn it back up with my right hand, taking a cleansing breath. Listening to the Irish music blaring instead of the whirring of hospital machines is refreshing. I lean my ever-tired head on the side of the door to watch my favourite shades of green run past us, racing us home. Before I can finish listening to the song, Mom interrupts.

"Oh! You have to listen to this song! It's called 'When You Believe.' I'm sure you've heard it before because I know you've heard this CD many times, but you must listen to it again. It talks about miracles. It makes me think of you and the miracle that you survived the car crash and are now learning how to walk again. You're so wonderful, my little miracle."

Yeah I'm a real miracle. You know what would have been a miracle?

Surviving the car crash without a brain injury, not having to learn how to walk again, and not having such a hard time in my difficult therapies. How pathetic I am, needing so much concentration to do such simple things. What would be a miracle, is if people could know and appreciate what they have without losing it first. That would be a miracle. The song plays anyway, although I'm not interested in listening.

As it plays, I start to make personal connections. Before I knew its complexities, my body used to do all these amazing things with little to no effort. I tense up as I think of the difficulty I have getting people to hear me with my soft voice. I snarl at the lyrics about seeking faith. No offence to the religious, but I'm not looking for faith right now. I am spending my days trying to get enough rest to have the energy to teach myself how to walk. I'm the one putting in the work here. I certainly don't feel a divine power helping me lift my arm any higher than I can do myself. I take a deep breath. All this work has been a lot harder on me than I thought. Just because life has been hard on me lately, doesn't mean I should put down faith. I believe in the power of hope and the power of people sharing their hopes with me.

Isn't that what prayer is? Hope for a better future, a better life. I might not care to pray for myself, but I certainly appreciate someone else offering to do it for me. It makes me believe I can get through this and return to some sort of ordinary life in society. *Believe, believe…* Okay, I guess it's a good song. It's like someone created a religious version of my life and wrote a song about it.

At home I find that all my practice has served me well. I move swiftly enough that Mom starts to loosen her grip on me. After proving myself, I ask her if I can try walking to the bathroom alone. I promise to hug the wall on the opposite side of the stairs and not go near them. I'm surprised when she agrees so quickly and easily. Making it to the bathroom on my own successfully, her eyes on my back, I glance into my bedroom. I can't wait to sleep in my own bed tonight.

Once back in the living room, I notice its new layout. When they heard that I was coming home, my aunts worked together to arrange a living space upstairs next to the kitchen. The open-concept kitchen already had a little space in front of it, which they transitioned into a small family room. A new couch now separates the room from the kitchen. They painted the back wall a light pine green, as an accent wall.

Much of the day was spent getting me here, but I'm here all weekend, so I'll make sure to start enjoying myself first thing tomorrow.

* * *

Getting in the car to go back to the hospital on Monday, I would kick and scream if I could, but I still don't have the energy to actually do it. Instead, I take one last step of freedom and a deep breath of fresh country air before I climb into the car. The whole weekend flew by. The stay included puppy hugs, mostly from Lindor, and visitors sharing meals. The new couch Mom had put in was much more comfortable than any other place I had been all summer. I even fell asleep there once or twice. Mom let the dogs up on the couch to cuddle with me, breaking a rule she has maintained my whole life. With the feeling of home among the country scenery, there was so much leniency, freedom, fresh air, and luscious, green openness.

Mom puts the same song on for me again for our trip back into town, but it no longer has the same meaning. Instead, I turn towards the beautiful, mid-summer Island landscapes zipping past—the spruce, the pine, the fields, the grass—full of nutrients and power. The last of the colourful lupins, the light blue sky, and the dandelion yellow all come together to paint my picture of utopia.

Arriving at the hospital, Mom drops me off in a wheelchair at the main door. I take advantage of these extra moments outside before returning to my cell. I can't believe it's over. When will I get to go home next? People can still barely hear me. My left hand is moving, but it's so slow, and my shoulder has begun to ache at times. My walking has been going well. There's even talk of transitioning to a regular cane. I might even practise walking on the treadmill and try walking for longer distances; I'll just stop on the sides of the treadmill if I need a break. There is so much to do; this will never end. I just want to go back home. Mom leads me, heavy headed, into the elevator to return to my room in unit seven. I try so hard to keep it all inside, just accept my fate and keep moving forward like I've been doing since I woke up.

Jesse walks past the elevator doors. She's with another patient, an elderly lady with a walking belt around her waist. It's the same one I've been wearing. "Oh! Kamya! You're back! How was your weekend at home?" Her smile is big and bright, and her curls flying everywhere.

And that's it, that's all it takes. I burst out into the loudest and saddest tears one could even possibly burst out. I make such an uproar, and as the elevator doors slide closed Mom gestures an apology. I continue to cry through the halls, back to my room. Mom and I pass many strangers, nurses, and even some doctors. At first, she's sympathetic, but I think she soon gets annoyed and embarrassed. Finally, after closing the door, she tells me I must pull myself together before the doctor checks in on me to see how my weekend went.

"We don't want him to think it didn't go well, because it did, but your crying will not reflect that." The thought of this calms me down a little. All I want to do is return home as soon as possible.

I find some composure by the time Dr. Bryan comes into the room—it doesn't last long, though. Once that dam bursts, it's hard to stop the flow. I've been so good at keeping it together this whole time—finding out I couldn't walk and learning how to do everything all over again, moving my dumb left hand and my dumb left arm, repeating every single frigging thing I say for people to hear me. I have been a good girl, holding it together this whole time, and that's all it takes—a short weekend home in paradise and a painfully short drive back to Charlottetown; the thought of that hard hospital bed, the wheelchair, the elevator; and all it takes is my physiotherapist, whom I love, asking me cheerfully how my weekend went.

The weekend was wonderful. It was so wonderful that it now makes everything else seem like hell. When my tears burst out again right in front of the doctor, I just can't help it. Mom shared a look with me, but I continue to cry as she desperately tries to explain to him that I am just sad to be back, but my weekend was successful.

Finally, she has to take him away from me so that I have space to cry and so he can hear her. She explains to him in detail that I have done a great job moving around and that the new setup at home works well. She didn't even have to give me the sleeping medication I take here at the hospital. I try to wipe away my tears and confirm everything she says. I also try to tell him the benefits of seeing my dogs and sleeping in my own bed. He ends his visit by telling me it is terrific to hear that my weekend was a success. He says he'll start talking to my therapists to see if we can make my discharge sooner rather than later since it's evident that I would much rather be home. I swear I can feel his relief when he finally leaves to finish his rounds with other, non-crying patients. Mom smiles at me, joking that maybe crying helped me get home sooner.

"That's not…" I blubber and pant, "why I did it."

"I know." She pats me on the back. I feel juvenile, but I am not ashamed for crying, I can't help it. Honestly, it feels kind of good to finally let something out.

She continues, "Hopefully, we can convince everyone that you're ready to go home and be an outpatient!" I sigh. *Yes, that definitely would be nice.*

Before the end of the day, the doctor comes back to reassure me that all my therapists have agreed to try and work for release. At that time, I'll return as an outpatient, where I go home to sleep and come into the hospital during the day to continue my therapies. They'll keep a room for me to rest during the day since rest is essential in my healing, but that's all the room will be for. This relief is new to me. I had no idea what being an outpatient would be like; perhaps like my weekend at home but without all of the crying after. Being home more often will be nice, and I like working with my therapists here. They're all so good to me, and we've been working so hard.

Much of our work in OT with Edith is focused on my left hand's fine motor skills since I got out of my sling. Progress is slow, but it's there if you look. She suggests I tie my right hand behind my back to force myself to use the left more. Since this obviously won't work for me, I convince her that I'll force myself to use my left hand more instead. Although I've successfully taught myself how to open a bottle with my right hand only instead of asking for help, I now have to either learn how to do it with just my left or use both hands together. My hands must start learning how to work together and support one another. I hate using my left for anything. I hate it to the bone and fight with Mom about it. Every time I try to do something with my right hand. She asks, "Why don't you try doing that with your left instead?" *Ummm, how about no.*

Speech therapy with Carlton is going much better. I'm getting the hang of making the correct vowel shapes with my mouth. My pronunciation and enunciation of words have improved so much that I can whisper complete sentences without too much thought. The problem, still, is volume. For this reason, I still use sign language and hope Mom can read my mind a lot throughout the day. My therapists are getting to know me well, making our communications easier. Jesse is probably the best at understanding me at the hospital. My guess is it's because we've spent so much time together. While I work on improving my volume with Carlton and my fine motor skills with Edith, I continue to work with Jesse to transition to a single-pronged cane.

When I officially start my days as an outpatient, my next goal will be to return to school for the fall. I've been given until the end of August to prove myself worthy. I will be a discharged patient at that point, and my life outside the hospital will truly begin. Carlton refers me to a vocal therapist who works at The Guild downtown. The Guild is a small musical theatre in Charlottetown, so I'm unsure what to expect. Being an outpatient opens the opportunity to accept help from outside the hospital. Still, this new type of therapist must work with stage performers, where volume is probably a common problem. The excitement of working with someone who's not in the hospital is intriguing. We make the arrangements for me to start regular appointments there. Meanwhile, my OT time will ensure I'm mentally strong enough to handle the course loads when I return to school. It saddens me to learn that OT will be my new dominant therapy over physio, but I'm sure I'll get used to the changes. The only reason I prefer physio now is because I'm there more frequently and so it's more familiar.

At The Guild, I wait to meet my new therapist, curious about what kind of work we'll be doing. I wonder how different it'll be from my facial exercises at the hospital. After walking through the theatre, I sit with a woman at a piano in her office. We don't start with any kind of official assessment. We just talk like friends and get to know each other. Her name is Julia, and she tells me about her family. Then she asks me questions about myself and my life. After a while, she explains she's been using our conversation to assess my speaking volume levels.

I speak slightly louder about things I'm passionate about, like my dogs and my anticipation to return to school. Using this, she knows my full capabilities and recognizes that I can speak regularly at that level. Still, though, my highest level is not so loud. She says my voice is very airy—as if I have the lungs for speaking, but I'm not pushing the air out strongly enough to kick my vocal cords into gear. Our focus will be to strengthen my diaphragm. I love that she takes the time to explain what's wrong, why it's happening, and how I can fix it. It feels so different from when I first met my therapists in the hospital with Mom. It's weird being a patient and just being told what to do, or at least, only understanding it in that way.

My new work in OT is primarily quiet, slow research, looking at various strategies for studying and memory. I go through big books with thick pages and large letters. I practise grocery lists, the best walking techniques, and number equations. We usually end with further exercises for my left hand. At first, I'm not worried about number equations since I did well with my math teacher's questions when he visited me. Still, I require extra time when Edith gives me seemingly simple word problems and questions that include analogue clocks and time. Working within a sixty-minute hour is a whole new type of math. It's something I'll need to practice more. I think about scheduling time, something Mom's been doing for me without me realizing. I have so many opportunities to practise this, so I'll try taking over the job of timekeeper.

*　*　*

Weeks before returning to school, I learn I'll have to do an official cognitive assessment to see if I'm ready to enter Grade 12. Physio has been doing very well with my physical progress. It's my new hope to walk into school, tall and proud, with no cane, no wheelchair, and no one holding my hand. I feel like I'm getting close. My vocal therapist, Julia, has been working with me alongside my morning appointments at the hospital. Soon, my mornings are filled with preparation for this assessment. I feel the need to ace it. I want to be able to go back to school so badly. A psychologist I've never met before will test me in parts rather than all in one day since I don't have the strength or stamina to work my brain that long without rest. I'm thankful everyone understands this since it's not something I can control.

On my first assessment day, the psychologist, Dr. Balliol, explains that she'll do her best to monitor how tired I am and to notice when to break for the day. That's good because I'm not great at measuring my fatigue yet. I feel all-in for one second, and then fatigue hits me out of nowhere and takes me out.

All the assessments are long and exhausting. The first two days include a lot of memorization—it's a good thing I've been practising my memory skills during my downtime. She gives me a list of many words to memorize, which I recite back in order as best I can. I manage the first few words easily, ones that stick out to me. I squeeze my eyes to try and bring extra blood to my brain, hoping that will spark a memory of the last words she mentioned in her list, but my mind often goes blank. *Isn't this why people write lists?*

After focusing on my next test, she asks me to recite the same list of words without any forewarning. I have no idea how I'm doing, performance-wise. There are some words I feel confident about, but I've felt confident about things before only to realize I'm sadly mistaken. I complete many tests, like word games, spelling a word, words that could be associated with each other, puzzles, math problems, and drawing shapes. Before I return to my room, Dr. Balliol asks me to draw the same shapes I drew in the morning by memory. I complete that task with no problem, or at least I hope so.

The next day, we work with clocks. I draw out a clock with the time given to me and repeat it blindfolded. I do my best, although I have no idea whether someone without a brain injury would be able to do this perfectly, either. It feels silly. Next, she says to draw five o'clock, and I do my best again. When I take my blindfold off, I'm quietly impressed. *That's not so bad. Sure, it's more like a Salvador Dali clock than one on the hospital wall, but you can clearly make out the time.* Dr. Balliol seems less impressed, however, and more focused on continuing the tests. She gets me to draw the clocks out several times, displaying a range of times. Finally, she lets me put it away and says we've finished the paper portion of my assessment. Then, we move to a computer.

She has the computer all set up for me and tells me that she understands watching the screen might be difficult for me, so we can pause or take a break whenever I need to. While this neuropsych test is certainly more than frustrating and angering, I can understand why it needs to be done. My mind is muddled with fatigue and disappointment, and I try only to focus on doing my best so I can continue heading in the direction of getting my life back—going back to school, seeing my friends, realizing what limitations need aid. I nod and watch and listen as she explains the rules of the computer test to me. For example, I need to press the spacebar when I see YES on the screen and do nothing when NO comes up. I've seen things like this before; I might have even done this test in school or playing online. It seems simple enough, but my worries about not being good enough grow with every mistake I make.

With that now complete and a couple of seemingly simple flashing screen tests, I can't help but let my mind wander off. She gives me a short break, but is it really a break if you can't turn off your thoughts? I think about the irony of staying away from screens to avoid overstimulation, to now look at nothing but a screen for what seems like hours for a test. It doesn't make sense. I know we discussed this right before these tests.

She's taking it into consideration while measuring my performance, but as it's a standard test, it's unavoidable. I wonder if this is a sign that I should be ready to start watching TV occasionally. What kinds of shows would I like to see again? Up until now, I've only been watching TV for a few minutes at a time.

Before the accident, I regularly communicated online with a guy named Matt in England. You could say we were dating; however, I haven't had much time to think about him since the accident. Because I met Matt through family friends, my aunt has been able to keep him up to date, but it would probably be nice to send him a little message to let him know that I'm okay. I won't be able to stay awake until two or three in the morning anymore, but maybe we could send more emails. I barely get through a day without a nap, and my nighttimes are precious. That's just another reason I'm so glad to be back home; I sleep better in my own bed. I'm sure my doctor also let me return home for that reason. I shake my head. I am *supposed* to be resting my mind, not congesting it with unnecessary thoughts. I take a deep breath.

"Are you ready to go now?" Dr. Balliol asks. "Just a little more to finish." I'm really not, but if I sit here any longer in this silence, I'll just take another loop through my thoughts. I want to finish. We've been at it for days, and I think people usually finish this exam all in one day. That's ridiculous. How can anyone do all this work in one day? But I continue. The sooner I can return to school and see my friends daily, the better.

Chapter Six: High School

I have a little extra work before my first day back at school. I assume I passed my cognitive exam, as no one has told me otherwise. I have to get settled with the new therapists I'll be seeing outside the hospital, not to mention work with Julia to ensure people can hear me when I raise my hand in class. Can you imagine how embarrassing it would be if the teacher had to pause the lecture to come over and put their ear to my lips?

To prepare for my life as a non-patient, Mom buys me a treadmill to practise walking. It has handles on either side, in case I need to catch myself, and a string to pull in case I fall. We set it up in the basement, which is perfect because it also forces me to practise the stairs.

On a weekend where my uncle isn't too busy, he takes me fishing on his boat to help make up for the fact that I wasn't able to attend this year's Canada Day celebrations. Canada Day is my favourite holiday, next to Christmas, because both include large gatherings with my family. However, Canada Day tops Christmas due to its unique location for our festivities—my uncle's fishing boat. North Rustico, PEI, is a small fishing village that's close-knit and old-fashioned. I attended school here from kindergarten to Grade 9 in the same building, and it's where I made lifelong friends from Cavendish to South Rustico.

Typically, all families in the surrounding area show up in North Rustico for Canada Day, alongside the tourists. The day starts with a large parade—which we all have been a part of at some point in our lives—followed by fun activities and booths in the park with live music from local talent. Next is a boat parade in the evening where local fishermen line up in their decorated fishing boats at the docks. It feels like almost a hundred boats parade into the harbour, each uniquely decorated in red and white and well-stocked with music and merry-making. Since most of the boats are already in use during this season, the fishermen have to come in early to spray and scrub their boats clean for the event. Together, the boats take a short trip into the bay, turn around, and return to the docks, all while waving to the onlookers standing along the harbourside. The community spirit radiates on this day. You can usually bump into people you haven't seen in years, smile, share a hug or handshake, and then move back to your group for fun in the sun. It's a delightful day, and I spent that day in the hospital this year. I wasn't even on PEI; I wasn't even conscious!

After a busy morning of charters, my uncle washes and scrubs his boat for a second time and is taking Mom, James, and me out so that I don't feel like I completely missed out. As I'm proudly climbing into the boat, everyone is around me with their hands up, ready to catch me if I fall. Once I'm aboard, they hand me my cool metallic orange cane and direct me to my reserved seat, the cool ocean breeze whooshing across my face. I take in the blue sky, the water, the wind, that magical line separating ocean and sky, all between fluffy white-water splashes and people I love sitting around me.

At home, after a day of splashing, chatting, and taking deep breaths with my family, I curl up and fall asleep in bed, comforted by the ocean air in my lungs and dreaming about when I asked my uncle Dale to speed up so I could feel the water on my face, and he didn't hold back.

I can feel myself heading back to a normal lifestyle. The boat ride felt like a reset, bringing me back to life. I now feel ambitious about doing some simple cooking. I was never a chef or anything, but Mom first taught me how to cook when I was probably five or six. It's something I enjoy and I feel it could give me a small sense of independence. I'm only slightly worried. *Will I forget something on the stove and burn it? Will reading the recipe tire me out before I can get to its end?* My confidence is weak, like my body. After learning the results of my brain injury, uncertainty poisons my mind and I can't shake it. I have to prove that I can do some simple tasks, like cooking, and still have some control over my life. And then, I do it! I cook breakfast and don't burn anything.

Vocal therapy is helping, too. Since working with Julia, my volume has improved significantly by strengthening my diaphragm, most often by singing. You need a solid diaphragm to sing well and at a high volume. Normally, we choose from her workbook and concentrate on songs that increase my pitch.

"For today," Julia starts, "I have a special song that reminds me of you and that you're so unique and strong. It's called 'True Colours.'"

"Okay," I say, hoping it's nothing like Mom's semi-religious song. I don't want anything too emotional. As this is one of my last visits with Julia, I don't want to break down now.

"Great! And then maybe after, you can pick a song for yourself to sing, anything you want, as long as I can play it on the piano. Sound good?" I nod, and she starts playing, singing the song for me first so that I know its melody.

I instantly love it. This song speaks to my soul. It understands me. It makes me feel accepted, and all at once, I start understanding that I'm not like everyone else—I'm different and unique and I need to show my true colours. I'm the only one who can measure my self-worth. People can see me as brave, strong, and resilient, but I can feel scared, weak, and uncertain. I shouldn't feel guilty about it. So I sing it, and I can feel that thing Julia told me when we first met about how you use more volume when it's something you're passionate about. By my third try, I'm belting the finish in a way I've never felt before. Hearing myself with such volume brings tears to my eyes. Even though I feel my voice can be annoying at times, I do have a lot to say. I haven't realized until now the fear I felt at the possibility of losing this ability to sing with happiness.

The song resonates with me. *It's right about everything.* Why am I hiding the fact that I'm tired, sore, weak, and afraid? I'm only lying to the world and making everyone think there's nothing wrong with having the left side of your body paralyzed. It's a lie! And what if someone were to put themselves in danger, not knowing the truth of what I experienced? I can't let the world think I'm okay when I'm not. I could be missing out on extra help that I could benefit from. All because of what? Because I don't want people to worry about me? Do I really want to face my problems alone after experiencing how powerful help can be?

If my family hadn't known my sadness for missing Canada Day, I would never have gotten that private boat trip. Suppose I didn't express with complete certainty that I wanted to return to school in September; who knows if I would've gotten the extra therapy that helped me get to this point. I wrap up our short meeting by picking out a song for myself: "Danny Boy," a classic for Grampie. Something to ground me again before I leave.

※ ※ ※

Mentally preparing myself to walk into a school in just a few days, I'm walking with Lindor on the dirt road, where the ground is softer for my feet and fewer people can witness my sometimes-troubled gait. We occasionally take Littlefoot with us, but he's sometimes more difficult to walk. Lindor walks freely next to me like I trained him, but I couldn't teach Littlefoot to walk without a leash. Mom is protective of him because of his megaoesophagus.

Today I decide to try running for the first time since the accident. You always see in movies people who are injured somehow, maybe even disabled like I was, in that scene where they run for the first time and feel free. I want to recreate that scene. Usually, the person goes dramatically from wheelchair to standing to running, but I know that part is unrealistic. I don't even remember when I first stood, or when I took my first steps. Running for the first time, though, with nothing and no one holding me up, that's something I will always remember. I wonder if I'd be able to do it. I walk with Lindor ambitiously up the hill and down another dirt road, where no one other than the occasional farmer ever went by.

"Okay, Lindor, you're the only one here," I tell him. "If I fall and hit my head on a sand rock or something, you run home for help, okay?" I laugh as Lindor gives me a sad, serious look. Sand rocks and prickly bushes are all I have to worry about on this road.

"I'm just joking, baby. I won't fall. I promise. Well, I can't promise that, but I promise I'll try not to, okay? I just need to try this." He stares, waiting for something.

It will be fine, and if I end up hurting myself, it shouldn't be so bad. This isn't something I would recommend anyone else trying alone, but I'm feeling confident in myself, my phone is safe in my pocket in case I need to call someone, and I'm not too far from home. At worst, I might get some red dirt on me, but then I'll have time to recuperate over the next few days before I walk into school. I start with little momentum. My calves feel weak and sore as I push forward to go faster. I figure I should start with smaller steps in place of larger strides. Free-falling into my next step will feel different with speed. It isn't so bad. My steps feel awkward, my ankles loose, and my head heavy, but I'm steady and not falling. My eyes start to burn a little from the cool, salty wind.

I don't make it far before the strength of my ankle begins to give out, unable to support the pressure of a free fall with the extra factor of speed. A sharp, pinching sting suddenly chases up to my right calf, and I soon have to stop. A well of disappointment buries itself inside my soul. I sniffle to try and mask it, but soon I smother it out. It gets replaced with anger.

Typical. I should've known this would be a problem. Movies are bullshit. They don't show the hours a person would have spent in therapy training. Nor do they even mention the plethora of other problems resulting from associative injuries. I may have spent most of the first month with a physiotherapist relearning how to walk, but still, on top of that, I was learning fine motor detail and speech therapy. Then, in my second month, I had most of my focus on returning to school, because that was the goal I set for myself. What do I know? Maybe the people in those stories only had to deal with one specific physical limitation.

Everything I've learned about human biology this summer tells it's never as simple as just one problem to fix. The brain and body are too complex, interwoven, and valuable to whittle down to a straightforward solution. They don't show the truth in the movies because the truth is it's slow. Painstakingly slow. Almost unrecognizable. You'd think going from not walking to walking would be fast and exciting, but it's not. It's mostly just depressing and a lot of work, with what seems to be a minimal outcome at the time. I shouldn't be thinking about how other people might have handled similar situations. I know my problem is unique, and only I can find my limitations. I'm glad I tried running. It was a limitation I had to push and now know more about. Now, I can confidently walk into school without help, maybe not even from a cane. It would be embarrassing to have my mom beside me, holding my hand through the school doors. Ugh. I don't want that.

On our way to school for my first day, I still haven't shared with Mom that I tried running, and honestly, I probably never will.

"I can't wait to walk in those doors without any help," I say to her, casually looking out at the road ahead.

"Are you saying you don't want me to come in with you?"

"No, certainly not. I haven't needed your help to walk in a while, Mom. So why would you think I'd want that?"

"Okay, so what do you mean 'with no help' then?" She asked.

"I mean, I want the cane to stay in the car." My face is forward, my voice clear and precise. She blows a raspberry in response.

"Oh, come on, you're not leaving the cane in the car. What would you do for the rest of the day? You still have to walk to your classes and take your lunch break."

"That's not the point. I want to do it. I have to do it. I have my dream of walking into school with no help—no cane, wheelchair thrown away." I drift off briefly and return adamantly. "I need to complete that dream. I don't know. I could hold onto walls or something."

"But how effective will that be? I understand you have your dream, and it's wonderful to have dreams, Kamya. That dream got you this far, but I cannot let you leave your cane in the car with me. I'm dropping you off and going to work. I'm not taking your cane with me." Mom chooses protectiveness rather than understanding. In a way, it shows her faith in me. She knows I can do it on my own, but today is her first almost-full day away from me. This insistence should be telling me what is going on in her head.

I see it a different way. She doesn't get it. Even if I make myself look ridiculous the rest of the day, completing my mission of walking into school is important. Or else, what has all this work been for?

When we get to the school, I walk out of the car with the cane and secretly lift it while stepping through the door. It's a cheap trick, but this way I have the friggin' cane in my hand while Mom watches, but technically, I walked through my school's doors on the first day with no help from anybody or anything.

The morning goes by smoothly. We have arranged for me to take two classes in the morning, and then Mom will pick me up to bring me back home for the rest of the day to do homework. When I have appointments, I will do them in the afternoons. I detest the cane, though. The fact that it helps me doesn't even cross my mind. It's a constant reminder of how much I depend on it. I can't trust my left arm to hold and guide it without looking or feeling unnatural, but my left shoulder isn't strong enough to carry my heavy books to class. I turn and ask my friend Loriann if she will carry my books for me, gesturing to my cane, feeling guilty about needing to ask anyone anything.

"Of course I can! No problem," she says cheerfully, swiftly taking my books and skipping next to me on our way to class.

"This is great, actually," she says as we start our journey. "I'm thrilled to help in any way I can. I feel so helpless knowing what you went through, and meanwhile, I'm just living my life normally. So doing anything helps me feel like I'm doing *something*, even if it's just carrying your books." I share a simple, thankful grin with her, feeling like I suddenly understand why people bake for others going through hard times.

I don't know if I've thought of that before. I've been so focused on myself, my restoration, and my problems. All I've thought of about anyone else up to this point is my gratitude, and I marvel that they are helping me when I can give nothing in return. Maybe that's what it is;

besides being for love, they just want to feel like they're doing something and not just watching me struggle. Loriann is already steps ahead of me. I walk independently but slowly. I still need to focus, so maybe it's better if I don't have anyone walking next to me chatting.

The first week of school goes well—as soon as other people start to see that I don't mind them carrying my books for me, everyone starts offering. One day, two friends even argue about who would get to carry my books. It feels nice to be laughing with my friends again.

The new setup at home is great. Mom and I spend more time watching TV together upstairs. At first, I am scared it might be smothering, but she makes it relaxing. She brings us snacks. We have some regular shows, like almost every day we watch *Ellen*. As soon as the clock hits six o'clock, we change the channel so that we can watch it together. It's an hour where we can forget about the therapies and homework and just have a laugh and be reminded of the good parts of life. We watch other shows too. Most of the time, it's just me accompanying her while she watches shows she likes. It has been so long since I watched TV, and who knows, maybe my preferences have changed. I worry my preferences in general might have changed due to the brain injury. The concept frightens me so much, I don't want to even test relying on my preferences. So, I let her take the reins, and I'll slowly relearn what I like and dislike.

In the middle of watching an episode of *The Ghost Whisperer*, I excuse myself to go to the bathroom. Mom jokes and tells me to hurry back before the commercials end since I'm still walking like a sloth. Usually, if I hug the wall to steady myself, I can walk faster, but I can't help but get this sense of danger within the darkness at the end of the hall. While walking into the dark hallway toward the bathroom, a deep hole emerges in my gut, and my eyes start to well up with tears. I blink hard because I know better than to think there's such a thing as ghosts, and I know better than to think one might be by the dark window at the end of the hall or coming out of Mom's bedroom. I don't understand where this is coming from. I never had a hard time with scary thoughts like this before. I want to cry with both confusion and frustration. None of this makes sense. Before I return to the couch, I speak up so that Mom knows I'm there just in case something grabs me from behind.

"Oh my God, Mom. I don't know how to describe it, but I *feel* like ghosts are at the end of the hall. I feel like it's a fact. *They are there.*"

"Oh wow, really? It must be because of all the ghosts in that show," Mom says gently, getting there a lot faster than I did.

"I feel like I could cry. I'm so scared. It's awful."

"Do you want to watch something else?"

"Yes, please. This has to be a brain injury thing. I just can't figure it out. It's too much for me right now."

"I know what you mean. This brain injury has been confusing for both of us. Do you want me to go look for ghosts for you?"

"No, I know there's no ghosts. I'm not a child. But this is why I don't understand where this is coming from!"

"Even in the hospital, I felt like I was constantly asking your doctor why certain things may be happening, like when we asked why you were having trouble remembering things from the day before. He told us it could be several things, but because brain injuries are so difficult to track that closely, it was almost always likely to be associated with either your brain injury or its process of healing. I wish they could tell us more about what to expect. No one could tell us anything because no one knew what to expect, so we were all learning along the way, but that doesn't make it not scary. It *is* scary. Because it's hard to distinguish between reality and your brain playing tricks on you. Even for me!"

She puts it so well here. Fortunately, I don't have to waste more energy speaking since she's spoken my thoughts for me.

Another strange occurrence has been happening in the shower. The water temperature dramatically changes when I spray the hand-held showerhead from my knees to my back. It's as if the water has a mind of its own. It'll be lukewarm on my knees and change to scalding hot on my back. The water doesn't understand that my legs are just fine; if anything, heat would be better for my leg muscles. But the extreme heat on my lower back is painful. Not sore like the area is tender, but *hot,* like it's burning my skin.

After our conversation about ghosts and Mom understanding my confusion, I feel like she might understand how the water changes temperature while I'm showering. I owe it to myself to see if it's all in my head. Mom believes me when I say I can feel the water changing temperature; she even stands there to feel the water and prove it's not changing. Of course, she has no answers. Instead, she tells me to explain it the same way to my therapists, and maybe one can give me a solution. I ask Lisa, my current physio, first since she's the next I see. She gives me some ideas of what it might be but suggests I ask my occupational therapist, Amber, since it might align better with her practice.

The next day when I see Amber, I do my best to explain my troubles. She reassures me that she's heard of things like this happening after accidents such as mine. Certain areas of the body can become temporarily more sensitive. It also makes sense to her that it's my back because I was in a car crash.

"Was your spinal cord injured in the accident?" Amber asks. "Maybe there is bruising or swelling, or your body is simply healing after such a large blow."

I think I remember telling her before that they told me my spinal cord wasn't damaged. It is my brain that gives me motor issues. I don't know how to explain everything again to make her understand. It doesn't matter; she's a professional and should already know this, so I quickly confirm what I remember. With all I know, and for all that I can trust this brain and body with, it could have become damaged after the fact, more recently. My difficulty with my short-term memory is constantly fogging details on me.

To solve my problems, she suggests I treat it like everything else. I should reteach my brain how to think correctly. She says I can feel the temperature on my legs and hands, making sure to keep it in mind. When I move the water to my back, even if it feels scalding hot, I'll know what it's supposed to feel like. Over time, my brain will learn to stop thinking of it as a threat. The whole idea is both frustrating and fascinating to me. It reminds me again how complex and confusing the brain and body can be. I try Amber's suggestion, thinking she's right and it can't hurt. At first, my back stings, but I slowly notice the burning sensation going away. Before long, within a span of a couple of weeks, the water just starts to cool down in temperature.

Over the next few months, normality returns further. I try standing in the shower instead of using the shower chair. This way, my whole body is under the water flow. I don't have to worry about my brain lying to me about the temperature changing—my hand and my back can simultaneously feel the water. I don't think of it as progress until I ask Mom if we can take the shower chair out of the bathroom since it takes up so much space. She is surprised and tells me she doesn't think I'm ready to spend the whole shower standing up yet.

"Mom, I haven't used the shower chair in over a week… I take it out, shower, and put it back in."

"Oh?" Getting quickly onboard, she says, "Okay then, I guess we'll put it in the basement." I laugh at her. I can see her feeling uneasy and going through an internal battle between making sure I'm safe and allowing me space to grow. I am glad her mind leans towards growth.

My therapists suggest I might benefit from a tutor for my classes.

When I have my appointments in OT with Amber, she usually goes through studying methods to help me find one that works for me and my memory. If I get a tutor, they could help me implement these different methods into my actual studies. Because I'm still nervous about what others might think of me, I take James up on his offer to tutor me. I won't have to hide my thoughts and feelings from him since he's already been through most of it with me. He stacks his university classes in the morning, so he has the afternoons free for me. When we aren't studying, he and his roommates let me watch TV with them, another touch of normalcy. It also allows me to spend time with people who are a little older and more mature. I'm starting to feel a gap in maturity between me and the kids at school. Not only in isolating myself socially to heal, but with what we choose to do with our free time. Some of my fellow students may be discussing the next party to go to while all I do is study, sleep, eat, and rest, with some physical training on the side. Hanging out with James and his roommates, I learn that this is what most university students do with their time, the nerdy ones anyway.

The mattress from my bed at home sits directly on the floor to be at a better height for me; I often sit there surrounded by my books. This is where I find myself staring blankly in front of me, caught up in thoughts. I feel like all I do is study for classes or go to therapy. I have no time for friends, no time to go out and do fun stuff every weekend. I can feel people around me buzzing and socializing, living 'normal' lives. I can't stop the wave of sadness mixed with frustration that comes over me, followed by memories of my time in hospital. I feel defeated. My ever-strong attitude from before my accident subsides into tears. I never used to cry like this before. Besides that time I lost it after my weekend pass, I've been keeping myself together pretty well, focusing on rehab and getting better. I haven't had enough time to dwell on the fact that I will never get back to where I was before the accident. But, sitting here, studying, and now procrastinating, I'm staring into the abyss, and it's all I can think about.

My mind gets flooded thinking of how much work I've put in so far, how hard it is to find anyone to relate to, and how impossible it is to explain my life to anybody. How can I explain what I'm feeling or how tired I am? I'm not only physically and mentally tired; my hopes and ambitions are tired, too. It's deeper than that, even. Everything tires me out. Even when I walk down the hall at home I need to close my eyes and take a deep breath when I get to the end. I am running on a dead battery but acting as if it's half full for the sake of everyone around me.

It's exhausting and impossible. How am I going to continue this? Speaking to someone or going to a support group is something I should likely consider, but my stubborn attitude of dedication and staying strong dominates. Leading myself into a panic attack, I can do nothing but stare into the air. I try to focus on the wall, but that's too much—I don't have enough attention in me. My battery is empty. *Okay, then stare at the air. Nobody says I can't stare at the air.* So, I do just that. I try to focus to see if I can look at the particles with my naked eyes. Of course I can't, but I soon realize I am focusing. I *do* have something left in me. I'm not back yet but I'm sick of staring at the invisible, empty, non-empathetic air. I want to do something that's not studying; I can't do that right now. I need to organize my thoughts and talk to someone who will listen and understand. But I feel no one can understand. The complexities of the brain after a brain injury aren't a concern in modern medicine. No one can help. I have to depend on myself.

Okay, I'll talk to myself then. No one's here. They won't know how crazy I am. I try to calm down. My heart is racing, my eyes darting around the room; I can't settle my thoughts. From what I've read, there are several ways to come out of a panic attack. I've been reading about them since I started experiencing some milder ones. I want to scream into a pillow, but my vocal cords aren't strong enough. That thought makes my heart beat even faster. I can't focus on any methods right now. *Why didn't I prepare myself further?!* I take a deep breath and try to start over. *Okay, forget other people's methods. What did you used to do when you wanted to sort out feelings or thoughts before the brain injury?*

It comes to me. A poem! Writing is healing. I used to love writing poetry; if I remember correctly, I think I am pretty good at it. I open my computer, search the thesaurus, and map out all of the feelings I've had since waking up from my coma. I put it plainly, not getting too deep into my problems. I sit back and cry. This is it. I feel the air in my lungs again. I'm unsure if anyone else would even relate to my poem, but I save it and hide it in a file for safekeeping. I finally feel a touch of understanding, even if it's just from myself.

My Thoughts

My thoughts are making me crazy
Even though it's hard to tell.
Only those who are looking
Notice I want to yell.

If only that were possible
My life would be that much better.
Since I can't, I need to find another way
And so I'm fitting it into this letter.

All I have for this moment in time
Is the future I foresee.
To have the patience for that time to pass
Is very hard for me.

People all around me
Are trying to imagine how I feel.
They'll never predict it right
Unless what they're thinking is real.

Writing this all down
Will not make it fine.
It will not be good again
Until I get back that wonderful life of mine.

Even though it's hard
I know I'll make it through.
You have to understand me to know
It's a thing I would definitely do.

* * *

We're returning to Moncton, where I spent about two weeks of my life that I have no memory of. I'm anxious to see if anything comes back to me. After a two-hour drive, with breaks to stretch all of my muscles, we arrive to meet with Dr. Meadows. Mom explains that he was my primary doctor while I was here and checked in on me almost daily. I only have one goal in mind when we get into his office: I want to get a picture of my brain. I want to see it and compare it to images of normal brains. We've been learning about the brain in my biology class, and I'm curious what a brain injury looks like in physical form.

Dr. Meadows gives me a bit of a timeline to focus on. He says a lot of my progress will begin to plateau around three years after the injury. After that, I will feel like I have a better idea of what kind of future I can expect. I'll try to avoid too much self-evaluation before then. Our visit is short and sweet. Mom certainly has more of a connection to the doctor than I do. As we're walking out, Mom asks me if I recognize him. I do my best to explain to her that I don't, but he seems like a great guy. It makes her happy enough. There's another fake movie scene: people waking up from comas and remembering everything that happened to them when they were unconscious. I don't remember anything that happened around me while I was in my coma. While I understand I was awake for a few days before returning to PEI, I still don't remember them. We'll probably never truly understand why.

This is all of little consequence to me; I asked for the MRI scan images I wanted. I'll print one and frame it someday, maybe put it up in my future office where people will ask me what it is, and I'll explain to them that it's an image of my brain after my injury. They'll be shocked to hear that I had a brain injury because I seem perfectly fine to them. Call it my vision board if you want. I plan this out as I'm getting ready for my morning exercise on the treadmill. I can walk much further now, almost over ten minutes. I often use music as inspiration. I can listen and sing to the music, so I'm practising my vocal exercises while also challenging myself to walk with less concentration. I can't focus on every step for the rest of my life. Eventually, I'll have to learn to walk like everyone else and let it come naturally. Even though I require less concentration than before, my left calf is still tight, and if I don't focus, I could easily trip on my toes. Not always, but the more tired I get, the more likely it is to happen. Therefore, I usually concentrate more than I'd like.

Listening to the music has helped. "Raise a Little Hell" by Trooper plays often from the inspirational playlist I made. I chose this song to help me get pumped up to walk and gain physical strength. Instead, I see myself, my poem, the image of my brain, and it does pump me up, but not energetically. It encourages me to plough through and continue my therapy and push for more progress even though times have been hard.

Oh, I'll be raising a little hell, alright. With shock, I smirk and suddenly realize that I've been walking without concentration on each step. Joy bursts out of me, and I need to stop walking to look around the empty, unfinished, unused basement for someone to celebrate with. *Haha, there's nobody here,* I realize. And that's how I like it. No one to judge me. Would anyone even understand this triumph? I'm sure they would if I explained it to them. It's the first sign that I can walk naturally without concentrating like some dingus as my reality threatens.

After experiencing what a good inspirational song can do for me, I turn back to my playlist. I want more songs like these. My mind goes back to when James told me he played music for me while I was in the hospital and how I told him I don't remember it at all; that music didn't mean that much to me. Now, it does. I search for new music, like I search the thesaurus when writing a poem. I use keywords, take some examples, and try suggestions. I try a few I think I can relate to: "I Just Wanna Be Mad" by Terry Clark, "Ain't No Mountain" by Marvin Gaye and Tammi Terrell, and a few more make the list.

* * *

On New Year's Eve, I look back at the mess I've experienced this past year. Going from the exciting adoption of Littlefoot to the first couple of real parties with my friends, to being in the accident, to rehab, to coming back home, to getting settled. It has been a wild ride, and I don't know what the future will look like. At seventeen, all I know is that I have to remain patient. I can't get through another year of progress if I start panicking now. No one knows what the future looks like, but if I could at least know how I'd walk, talk, or study, that would be nice.

Where will I be in a year? In ten years—the year 2020? It sounds big and important now, but it's just like any other year. Taking into consideration my rehab, I know the future is very uncertain. I could be running marathons by then, for all I know. Aliens could invade the world or we could experience a plague.

I continue my classes in the new year and meet with the school counsellor to explore my options. They suggest this for every student, but it's a little more crucial for me. I'm thankful to find out that my grades from before the accident were good enough to even out my average for this year. Even though most of my attention has been elsewhere, I still qualify for university. I leave the office with pamphlets, brochures, and bursary application forms, few of which fit my life. With my inability to work last summer, my university fund is lower than I would like. There's a bursary for students with disabilities I will look into. I'll only have time to apply for some of them—it turns out that applying for bursaries and scholarships can be a full-time job. Ever since I can remember, I've wanted to go to UPEI. Unlike many kids my age, I've always wanted to stay close to home. My dream is to attend UPEI, study psychology, take classes at the vet college and to become an animal behaviourist. It is a simple plan, and even though things might have changed, it's the one I'm sticking with for now because it's all I have.

This year involves a lot of looking at the future. I must now get evaluated to see what hours I can work this summer. I'll be working. I have a job, but I need to figure out how much of this job I can do and how much more money I can save. So, I'm spending my afternoons completing tests with a physiotherapist who can judge if I'm physically ready to go back to work and for how many hours. I've never met her before, so initially I am worried she'll work me to my limit, but instead, as soon as she notices my left side starting to lag or slow down, she asks me to stop and move on to the next physical task. I pick up a crate with a certain amount of weights in it and move it back and forth across the room. When I finish, she adds more weights and has me repeat the process until she tells me she's satisfied. By the end of the day, though, I'm exhausted. It doesn't matter if she isn't pushing me to my limit in each task. By the end of the third day I feel dead. I guess I can do okay in a day, but now whatever I do one day follows me into the next.

When she asks me how I'm feeling, I admit that I am tired, but can she really know how tired? By the time I'm ready to accept it, I'm usually at the point where I'm past tired and bordering on delirious. If I notify her when I'm tired, I'll have to start that way. I am always tired. I want to try to communicate that, but I don't know how.

I need to turn in a more positive direction once my physical examination is complete. I have done well enough in my classes this year to know I'll graduate and go to prom. The guy I was dating from before the accident, Matt, plans to travel from England to take me, so I'll need a nice prom dress. He's so romantic!

I let Mom make all the plans, and we go to Montreal to dress shop. All concerns I had about how my brain might react to the pressure of the plane proved to be nonsensical. Our cousin Eva greets us in our hotel room the following day with gourmet cupcakes from one of her favourite bakeries. We spend the weekend visiting different shops and restaurants. I find a royal blue dress to wear to my prom that's strapless and silky. It has a bit of mesh fabric in the front, making the strapless aspect more conservative. The moment I put it on, I feel like a princess.

Mom convinces me to attend my graduation ceremony when we get home, and my family throws a party to celebrate the end of my tough year. It'll be our last party with James before he leaves to go across the country for further education. The prom is beautiful. I helped decorate with an under-the-stars theme. We take lots of pictures. Finally, I start working part-time back at The Toy Factory, as we planned in our visit at the hospital, with a promise from my fantastic employers that we could adjust my hours as I saw fit. It feels lovely to be back in the shop. While I can't make toys as much as I used to, I can still smell the warm wood and sort through the colourful aisles.

Mom breaks the news that I'll soon have to go for another test—a neuropsych evaluation—to measure my progress since my review in the hospital. We're hiring a neuropsychologist off the Island and must travel to Halifax. This session will be with a stranger who knows nothing about me other than what's in my file, and I'll do it all on the same day. I've chosen to not take the opportunity to take the test across multiple days, because if I'm taking the test, I may as well do it properly.

I wake up in the Halifax hotel bed and start my day optimistically—I've made it through everything else. What's one more test? It's just another small step before I start university and advance into my future. Completing the test isn't a prerequisite to starting university. That will be a separate adventure, but I think knowing where I stand after a year post-brain injury will be helpful. Since it's so slow, I don't get many chances to see or measure my progress. Still, the differences will hopefully be significant enough for me to notice after a year. I get through the day—painstakingly.

When Mom picks me up after the test, the pressure of the day hits me like a train. I am exhausted and drained. I feel dumb. *A way to measure progress? More like a way to prove how inadequate I am!* Today's tests were similar to the ones I vaguely remember doing last year, but when Mom asks me if there were any new ones, I can't exactly remember. They were more frustrating tests of remembering short lists, word association games, and drawing shapes, this time with an assistant instead of the neuropsychologist. While she seemed friendly and cordial, she also seemed to be more interested in getting through the day than noticing how I was doing. I got breaks, but nothing felt like it was enough. How I feel now answers my question about how I'd ever be able to do these tests in one day. It's unrealistic. I don't know, maybe it's something that could be more realistic for the average person. I feel like maybe I'm just stupid. After staying silent in the car for as long as I can, I burst into tears, finally answering Mom's questions about how my day went.

"How dare this test make me feel inadequate!" I yell as loud as I can. "I was not only pushed past my limit but pushed out of my own body. I feel like I have no control. I can only imagine how dumb I've turned out to be. It's not fair that after all the progress I made this year, and all the work I put in, making it back to school on time, *graduating* on time. After all the work I put in physically to walk with a cane and then with no cane. Only to walk up the stairs after a long, draining day to finally see the psychologist and hear him explain when I can expect my results. Now, all I can do is assume and hope that he'll be able to convey them correctly in his paperwork, because I don't know how that works!" My fatigue has weakened my voice, so I'm unsure how much she understands.

She answers me with logic.

"Okay, first of all, no one *forced* you to do this test." Softening, she includes, "And you can only do what you're able to do, Kamya. And it's finished now. So, you're right. We can only hope he can report your results accurately."

If you think that's going to help me, you're wrong. My eyes are too angry and hot for tears to fall. My anger continues in silence. I rant quietly in my mind all the way back to the hotel because now I have no choice but to stay another night. A three-hour car trip from Halifax would be way too much to add to whatever is going on with me. I didn't know that this test was meant to be so draining! No one told me it was supposed to be like this. I guess no one would voluntarily take that kind of test. I don't care if Mom's right—I feel terrible.

My spirits are down, making me feel stupid and like a failure. My neuropsych abilities are pretty freaking scarce, according to what I experienced today. I'm so tired. I'm a strong person. I've made it *so far*. I'd like to see anyone do what I did! With as much freaking grace! Actually no, I don't want to see that. No one should have to go through what I did. That's too much to wish on anyone. It takes a while to calm down, and the food that Mom orders is helping. I shock myself with how much hate is in my heart. I can't watch TV right now; that's too much. I ask Mom that she doesn't watch it either. I just can't handle it. I cry myself to sleep while repeating that the test is over now, and I'll start classes soon.

Chapter Seven: University

Crossing the threshold of my very first apartment, unbalanced by the bags in my hands, I duck down as if I'm too tall to fit through the door. Instead, I look silly walking through a door that's not wide enough for my bags. This whole living-on-my-own thing is way bigger than I am. Thank God I found two friends from high school to move in with temporarily, Kristy and Loriann. We'll all take classes at UPEI and hopefully find a way to live and study together. I've seen my brother do it, so how bad can it be? I will be walking to school independently. I sigh. *Remember when I couldn't walk that distance? And now I will be doing it every day, with books!*

I feel a sense of accomplishment mixed with that feeling I'm sure every kid gets when they first move out. A sense of maturity mixed with false maturity. A feeling of certainty mixed with uncertainty. I don't know how it'll work, but I know I can't afford it not to. I *need* my independence. Now, I'm finally getting the opportunity to face the world on my own two feet, literally.

Waking up for my first day of university classes is a replay of this experience. One of the most exciting things about university is choosing which classes to take, the ones I will build my future with. I start my first year with biology, psychology, and anthropology. My caretakers and I have decided that I don't have the energy or mental capacity, I suppose, to take a full course load, so at least to start, I'll have three classes and will go from there. Maybe I can negotiate more later so it doesn't take me much longer than my friends to graduate. To become the animal behaviourist I always dreamed of being, I'll aim for a major in science with psychology. I chose biology for its science credit and anthropology as my one elective for the year, hoping it would be my fun course.

When looking in the mirror to prepare for the day, one word comes to mind: *different.* That's right, this year is going to be different. *Forget the makeup, then,* I think to myself, *nobody has time for makeup when they're dealing with a confused jumble of medical problems, adult problems, adolescent change, and the medical problems that I have!* Oops. I said medical problems twice. Repeating and forgetting things are now commonplace for me after my brain injury. *Oh well, that's probably because I'm considering my learning disability and fatigue as two separate medical problems.* I touch my forehead and mock headache. *It's too early for this.* I fling up my good hand at myself in the mirror for being dramatic and walk away. Even with a cluttered mind, it's still a new year, a new me. There is no need for makeup. These people don't know me, so I can be whoever I want.

The first few weeks of classes go like clockwork. The walk to school is far enough that it's an easy decision to just stay on campus between classes, and when I don't have classes, I schedule therapy appointments. Physio, massage, and occupational therapy; classes, lectures, labs, and private studying. Don't forget the crucial need to make time for naps. I'm lucky that I don't care what people think, so when I need to spend my days at school between classes, I just find a comfy chair or sofa and take naps there. Chronic fatigue is just that, feeling tired all the time, even if you've had an adequate amount of rest. Don't even get me started on what level of tired I can feel during times of less rest! That's when my body starts shutting down because my brain only has so much energy to steer me with.

Before long, I resume the driving lessons I almost completed before the accident. I'm learning from a different instructor now, one with more experience with brain damage. Her name is Heather, and she has experience teaching stroke victims how to drive again. Much of her experience has been working with elders. PEI is a small place; there's not much opportunity for different experience levels, but we do have a large ageing community here. A part of me feels disadvantaged. Does it matter, though? Experience is still experience. Knowing how an injury to the brain can change someone's functioning and teaching them how to work with that is the point. I only have to do these lessons for a short bit anyway. I was only about a month from getting my licence before I was forced to pause.

"I was able to see you last time and observe you pretty well," Heather starts when I get into the car. "It's obvious you know how to drive and remember what you learned a year ago, so that's great. We'll focus on your practice and getting used to doing things more safely. That way, you can feel more comfortable driving after your brain injury." She continues, "We're going to practise stopping almost before you stop so that if you need to stop sooner than you were expecting in the last second, you can. As I'm sure you know, individuals with brain injuries can have a little lag sometimes and can't react as fast. So, you should keep an extra distance between you and the car before you. That way, if the car stops unexpectedly, you have more time to notice it, react, and stop your car. Managing your spaces between cars will help you a lot, both with confidence and to avoid accidents."

When I'm at the apartment, I study on my bed. It's private. I can shut my door and forget everything else—at least until my mind hears silence and decides to end it with *infinite thoughts*. I start thinking about my plans for tomorrow in therapy. *When will I be able to study? When can I schedule my needed naps? When will I eat? What will I eat? Do we have food in the apartment, or should I ask Mom to pick up something on our way back from therapy?* Therapy. *What if I suddenly can't walk tomorrow?* My eyes start to tear. I distract myself with thoughts of how far I've come with the help of therapy and how much my exercises have contributed to my progress. I throw my heavy book away from me. This isn't going to work.

I hold my head in my hands. The headache is starting to feel real now. I've had a lot of never-ending thoughts like this since my brain injury. I feel myself spiralling downwards into a hole that has no place for me to study. While my mind has brought me to biology-adjecent thoughts, they have nothing to do with the type of biology I'm trying to learn. And you're supposed to know the basics to understand the complex, right? *You know what, music has helped my life before, so maybe it can help me again.*

I pull my computer closer, start it up, and do an empty search for music to help me study—a search where I don't look for anything in particular. Finding something will be tricky. I can't pick songs I know, or I'll just start singing along. I don't want to choose a song that won't suit the studying rhythm either. After tying my search in a knot, I settle on Elton John's *Greatest Hits*.

After having Elton John as a study buddy a few times, I'm thrilled to learn he's the absolute perfect companion. After that, I only stop studying a few times. Once, to research why his voice feels so familiar (it's because he sang the soundtrack for *The Lion King*—I am a millennial kid, after all). Another is when I start singing along to "Benny and the Jets" (yes, I'm listening to it enough to learn the words without realizing). And yet another time is to see if I can find anything else

(I don't find any). Eventually, I find the perfect studying rhythm I've been seeking.

Bursting through my door to interrupt my studying is my roommate, Loriann. She sits on my bed without invitation, bouncing up and down and ready to start a conversation with me.

"I can't study anymore!" she says, dramatically throwing her hands up into the air. "I just can't. The words are starting to blend, and I can hear Kristy playing a video in the room next door."

A couple of weeks ago, Kristy made the courageous decision to drop out of university, and instead use the rest of the year to discover her new path. I'm proud of her getting off a path that doesn't suit her, but I also can't help but notice that it changes the whole dynamic of the apartment. If we were all in university together, we would prioritize studying. That's how I thought it would be when we first moved in together, but it's okay. We'll just have to find a different dynamic. Besides, we only agreed to live here for the first year. I don't think I can afford a second year on my own.

"Anyway!" Loriann continues. "I decided to come and bug you. If I need a study break, maybe you do too!"

"Oh, thank God," I say. My exhausted eyes roll to the back of my head, and I plop my book and notes on the floor. She is right; I one-hundred-percent need this. I smile big and say, "Okay! What are we going to do instead?!"

"I don't know," she says as she picks up the wooden pencil holder by my bed. It's filled with crayons and in the shape of a transport truck; one I got from working at The Toy Factory. She grabs a crayon and starts doodling directly on the wood. "Maybe we could just talk."

I laugh nervously. "I don't know what we could discuss. I don't want to talk about my therapy." Already, I'm feeling some weight come off my shoulders with this study break. "Honestly, I don't know how you study in silence. I have to play background music to stop myself from getting distracted by overthinking."

"Oh! I know what you mean! But I can't play music because I just start singing along to it in my head."

"Oh my God! Me too! But I started listening to Elton John! He's got wonderful music, and I can just have him on in the background. It's so soothing."

"Oh really?! Play me something!"

I quickly decide not to play her "Benny and the Jets" since it's lately become my weakness. Instead, I pick a slower song that gives comfort but doesn't distract you from what you're doing.

"I think you'll like this one!" I put on "Sorry Seems to Be the Hardest Word." We listen to it for a bit, and before it ends, Loriann tells me she likes it a lot.

"He's right!" she says. "Sorry is a tough word for some people. Even when that something isn't your fault! Saying 'I'm sorry that life has been so hard on you' can be very difficult because sorry doesn't fix it, you know?"

"You're right," I say, slowly nodding. This comment relates to me and how I think people must feel around me. I feel a bit self-absorbed. I add, "Saying sorry can feel so heavy just because while attempting to be helpful, it's also just a word and can be useless. Ugh. I hate that university and living and stuff makes me think deeply about the world and people!"

"Oh, really? I love it." Loriann says.

Me too, but honestly, it's just another thing to occupy my thoughts, which I don't really need right now.

As fast as she sat down, Loriann gets back up again. "Well, I guess I better get back to studying. I hope you like what I did to your truck! I guess it's in crayon, so you can't erase it. If you don't like it, I'll just get you a new one. I'm sorry." I nod and looked down at the truck with its colourful scribbles, which include three stick figures with hair and a few other drawings of random objects.

"What is it? What did you even draw?" I laugh at her.

"It's us! That's me on this side, with all the things I think represent me, and you're on the other side with all the things I think represent you. And then James is the one driving. I guess that might not look like James. I added the red hair, but I think I've only met him once or twice. I'm sorry. Maybe if I put his name, it will be clearer." She grabs a random colour and starts working. Meanwhile, I'm laughing my head off, my sense enhanced by my being overtired. The stick figure looks like my brother enough.

I continue to ask her for details about which images she chose to draw, but after I see that she's written 'James Express' on the front of the truck, I lose it.

"Oh well. See you later!" And she's gone like the wind.

What a lovely little study break. I beam to myself, staring at the closed door behind her. Loriann and I have been friends since she moved to the Island when she was younger. It's nice to take a break from life and enjoy simple laughs with the people you love. I pick up my books and start where I left off but with some extra air in my lungs.

Kristy, too, has been one of my best friends for most of my life. Before moving in together, she and I decided to get our first tattoos together. I chose a tattoo that I had my heart set on since I was fourteen: a mayflower, just like the ones Grammie used to pick. I'll be happy to have a tattoo reminding me of my wild childhood, how Grammie could get me to sit still by putting some mayflowers in one of Grampie's old juice glasses in front of me. Their beautiful aroma was always intoxicating enough to keep me there. Having Kristy with me to get this tattoo representing a part of my childhood is fitting since she and my life with her were integral to that special time; one that's now gone, but I cling to as much as possible.

*   *   *

My occupational therapist, Amber, works tirelessly to try and find a study method that works best for me. We go through lists and different ways to memorize ever since we learned I'd be attending university—the power of visualization, repetition, association, anagrams, time management, etc. Then we do it all over again but change one small aspect to see if that improves things. I know that my appointments with Amber have been helpful for me. With this help, I've found a personalized study method works best. Instead of using only visualization or repetition, I write things down and organize them on paper to visualize later. Then, I'll go over the page repeatedly. It takes time, though, and it's not long before I realized how heavy a three-class course load can feel. I temporarily memorize stupid little details in OT, and then I go home and still spend the rest of the week memorizing things for the classes I'm actively taking. It's frustrating.

I still enjoy small study breaks to rest my brain, taking ten-minute naps and watching music videos. I've been ignoring newer music that became popular around my healing and ignorance. Starting the video for "If I Die Young" by The Band Perry, I immediately love its calm melody. I lean my head back and close my eyes. I'm so drained with school and everything, which is one of the reasons for this study break. The slow and calm melody feels relaxing. I concentrate on the poetic lyrics, as I often do with most music. The song is a story of a woman pondering what life would be like if she died at a young age.

Sixteen is a young age, I suddenly realize. *And it's the age when I almost died!* It dawns on me that with all the focus on making sure I get better and make progress, I haven't had the time to consider that I was in an accident! I almost died! A part of my brain *did* die; it's nothing but a white inkblot on the scans. I can't help but wonder what my funeral would have been like.

Suddenly, I start bawling and can't stop. The tears are coming so fast that I don't know how to wipe them away. I immediately feel the need to reach out to someone and seek comfort. I grab my phone, but there's still no one I can think of who can understand me right now. I don't want sympathy, and I don't want help. I don't want to see that look of pity, the unsure motions of their body while they wrap me in an awkward hug. I look down and think as hard as I can through my flowing tears, and it dawns on me. I wasn't in that car alone. Another of its passengers is right down the hall. I make my way to Kristy's room. We've been growing a little distant lately because I'm so busy with my studies and therapy and barely come out of my room. Regardless, we're still like family, so I bust into her room and walk cautiously toward her.

"I was just listening to that song 'If I Die Young' by The Band Perry," I anxiously tell her, trying to grab her attention away from her computer.

"Oh, I love that song!" She looks at me and it's like I can see her heart drop. She puts her computer aside. "What's wrong?! That's a beautiful song. Did something else happen?"

The room is now quiet. Her bed is neatly made besides the fact that she's currently sitting on it. Her room is the same shade of off-white as mine, but with a larger space around her bed. Looking down, I try to gather myself and figure out how I'm supposed to explain what's going on in my head. Without sugar-coating it, I take the most obvious route and do my best to communicate my feelings fast. The ceiling light hurts my tired, wet eyes. When I finish, I look at her desperately.

"I'm so sorry! I don't want to put my problems on you. And I don't want you to start thinking the same thing too now, but I just thought that maybe, since you were in the accident too… maybe you'd know where I'm coming from." I'm crying now, feeling guilty for putting her in such an emotionally charged situation. She looked like she was having a nice relaxing time before I came in, listening to music alone in her room.

"*I do!* I do know where you're coming from. I had a moment like this, too. Of course, mine was a lot closer to the accident when you were in the hospital. It might've even been while you were still in your coma. I completely understand that it took you so long to get there. You've been very busy." She stands up and grabs me into a deep, confident hug.

"But you have to look at it rationally, Kamya. It's almost a good thing that you're only realizing this now. Now that it's almost two years later, you *know* what the results of that accident are. I'm okay, living and breathing. And you're okay. I haven't talked to Hanna in a long time, but she's also out there living her life. You've learned how to walk again! I was there with you in the hospital when you attempted to take those first steps! You've come so far, and you're so brave. It's not like you've run out of courage, either. That's just who you are. You might still have a while to go, but I *know* you'll be able to do it! I do not doubt it. You're a wonderful person, and please know that if you ever need someone to talk to, I'm right down the hall."

I begin to cry harder. "Thank you. Thank you so much." With guilt-filled tears in my eyes, I debate asking her if she will just hold me until things start to calm down, but there's no need, she does it anyway. I take a few deep breaths, and it doesn't take long before the moment passes and I can go back to my room.

* * *

On campus, the Webster Centre, where students who need extra help studying go, starts to feel familiar. I take my exams here. It's in the same building as the library, so it's hard for me to feel out of place. I often nap in the library on armchairs placed together for students to study in and then go to do a midterm or final exam. I get time and a half to compensate for my slower recall. I also have access to a private or semi-private room to complete the exams in, so I don't have to worry about getting distracted by people shuffling and making noise. Instead, I get distracted by my breathing, and there's almost always a ticking of a clock somewhere, whether in real life or in my head. My OT, Amber, observed that I do better with memory recall when I don't have too many distractions. I'm very grateful and surprised the university can accommodate this for me.

 I take a deep breath in this chilly but not cold exam room. I can hear my blood pumping with anxiousness to get the answers right. My throat swells as the reality of my situation hits me again. Repeating thoughts of how tired I always am, how I've been put in a room alone as if I'm quarantined from the rest of the world; then, finally, after I finish this test that's been my focus these past few weeks, I still must go to therapy tomorrow and continue living my complicated life. I swallow. *Don't go down this rabbit hole now; it's not anything you haven't already come to terms with.* Tilting my head, I make the most exaggerated, wimpy sigh as my chronic fatigue takes hold.

 I need to sleep and stop studying for once in my life! I need to be free from this therapeutic prison I've put myself in! Just to live and breathe with no new problems hanging over my head. Does that even happen? Is that a thing? I close my eyes for a few seconds. Thank God I have the extra time to throw a crisis into this exam and thank God no one is in this room to hear my most pitiful sigh. *Should I give up? No! I've come so far.* With my smaller course load, I can't help but feel like I should be at the same level as any other student, but I'm not. It makes me feel pitiful.

These types of thoughts are constantly in my head, so I'm used to ignoring them by now. I quickly finish my exam and walk out just before my time is up.

*   *   *

I make an appointment with a counsellor to review the semester. I'm relieved to know that I passed all my classes. It's a big feat to make it through my first semester. The study methods I do at home are paying off. *Of course, how the hell do I tell that to a university counsellor who's used to helping students with problems like busy course loads, medical anxiety, or whatever normal problems normal people have. Family issues maybe?* I am completely blind to the fact that other people my age might also have life changing problems they're dealing with. I don't know. Fuck. *Damn, I shouldn't use the F word.*

It's tough to advocate for good mental health right now. I have to be serious about that, though. What doctors have warned me about seems scary, that association between cognitive decline and suicide can sometimes be expected in people with head injuries or mental abnormalities. I understand it now. I get it, and I see where I need to be careful. But do they know that it's not the freaking head injury that does it, but rather the stress of life that comes with the management and the fact that I don't fit into society anymore? Society seems oblivious to the fact that people are all different and don't all come from the same perfectly working machine.

Rest, now. I need rest. As my mind spirals, I get distracted and trip over my foot on my way out the library door. I do my best to recover gracefully and not attract attention. My memory goes to when I tripped on the treadmill in the gym. A small but bulky young man working with weights nodded at me to see if I was okay. That was so embarrassing. My face reddens at the recollection. Thank goodness Mom is picking me up today so I don't have to walk home. I think I'm going to the country this weekend, too! Some country air by the sea will be nice.

After a nice nap in some open space in the country, my head will be clearer, and I'll think more about how my feeling overburdened is becoming more serious. I can't keep going through spirals like that, especially during an exam. I consider ways to fix this. Right now, I use the gym at the university, then do exercises at home, and finally do those same exercises and stretches at physio every week. It seems excessive. So, next time I see Lisa I will ask her about this and negotiate something new. She agrees that as long as I continue my exercises and stretches at home and stay active, then I should be able to see her less often. That's one less appointment every week.

This helps me breathe for about a week or so until I realize that I've been doing the same type of juggling with OT, tutors, classes, and private studying. So, I bring up the same conversation with Amber. She helps me make a similar adjustment, allowing personal study and lessons to replace my frequent OT appointments and having them less often.

This gives me some more air and space to move. I feel less compressed. It works out so well that soon, I see no purpose for OT anymore, or tutoring either. When I mention this to Mom, she thinks I'm giving up. I shake it off, but it makes me nervous to tell Amber my decision. To my relief, she agrees.

"I do have some more study ideas and methods that I want to explore with you," she starts, "but most, if not all, are technological aids and programs on the computer. Since technology doesn't seem to work as well for you, I think we can feel safe setting those aside. However, if you decide you might benefit from them later, you have my number, and we can pick up where we left off. You seem to have a good schedule now, and you've passed all your courses so far! I'm not worried about you, Kamya. However," she adds, "I'm still a little worried about your ability to juggle all of life's demands. Would you agree to go and see a psychologist about this? To talk to and maybe help you organize appointments and studies?"

I think about this for a second. I don't need help organizing my life. I'm great at organization. I just need less to deal with. Days are only so long, and I only have so much energy. But I can't refuse to see a psychologist. Wouldn't that make me crazy? I like trying new things to see if they'll work. So, I agree to start seeing a psychologist in the new year before my next semester starts.

* * *

Over Christmas break, my dad and James both come to the Island, so we're together for the first time since I started rehab. Our visit starts tremendously well and feels normal. James has been studying in Vancouver, doing his master's in physics at UBC. I'm feeling excited and optimistic. Dad, James, and I are going to town later today to do some errands, get a special lunch, and go for a drive. Dad likes to go around and see the Island while he's here. I don't blame him, but I wish he'd enjoy its richness more than concentrating on what's changed. This new building here, that new spot there. He doesn't even care about visiting these new places. He just likes to observe them and tell us repeatedly, "That wasn't there ten years ago." I shake my head and smile at the thought of him doing that again today.

Before my parents divorced, they lived together in PEI. Aside from the physical distance we now have between us, he has always been here for me. My dad calls me regularly to catch up on my life. He offers wisdom when he can, and really understands that I get much of my personality from my mom. My sense of humour though, I would say I get from both of them. They both have a childlike enjoyment for life, although Dad probably displays this more freely than Mom does. He cracks dad jokes whenever the opportunity presents itself, and like any old man does, he often reminisces about how life has changed so much compared to when he was younger.

I notice Mom has picked up the mail, so I sort through the envelopes on the table as I try to come up with ideas for the day so it isn't entirely spent looking at new buildings that didn't exist over a decade ago. I stop when I come across an envelope for me. It's a letter from UPEI. I head back to my bedroom to open it in private but before I can shut the door, I read the words 'Academic Probation.' My life for the past year flashes before my eyes. *All this work. All of it. For nothing?! What?!*

After taking a moment, I carefully read it in full. The letter explains that my marks aren't high enough for their satisfaction even though I passed all my courses this year. This letter is a warning that if I don't improve next semester, they can put me on academic probation and suspend me from continuing to take classes next year. *But I passed my classes. I succeeded. I did what I had set out to do.* I didn't know that there was a grade requirement that would tell the university that I was serious about my education. Nobody told me about this. *They probably don't usually have to tell people about this because people aren't as dumb as me. Fuck, fuck, fuck, fuck.* The curse words are flowing now. *Are you fucking kidding me?! Do you even fucking know what I've had to go through to get here?* As I feel myself slowly, finally, breaking, Mom walks past my open door.

"Are you excited to spend the day in town with your dad?" She cheerfully pops her head into my room. "Oh wow, are you okay?" I hand her the letter without a word. I am speechless.

She reads it quickly, sits down and puts an arm around me.

"Don't worry about this, Kamya. This is a system to weed out the students who don't care about school and don't think they need to study to pass their classes because that's how they got through high school. You *did* study. I don't think any student has worked harder than you. Even when you come home for a study break, you're in this room with books on your lap. I can only assume that's how you fall asleep."

A smile breaks through my tears when I answer her. "I don't. I'm always good at putting my books aside before taking a nap or resting. I wouldn't risk losing where I am in my reading. But I don't know. *All* of the students try hard. Everyone is walking around campus tired. Maybe I don't try hard enough. Maybe I should be staying up all night studying." I look down at my feet, socks on, ready to go out and pretend my life is normal. Who am I even fucking kidding?

"But all the other students don't have to go to therapy every week, go to the gym, and read things repeatedly like you to remember. Some kids read it once and remember it immediately." I look at her strangely, my face still skewed with pain.

"I don't know what you know about university and studying, but I can tell you that most students aren't like that," I tell her. I roll my eyes.

"My point is," she continues, "they aren't trying to learn how to walk again. They aren't managing busy schedules like you are. They don't need to nap every couple of hours because they don't have chronic fatigue. The university knows this and won't put you on academic probation. If they do, I'll help you fight it."

"I nap more often than every couple of hours." I laugh for a little bit through the tears, which feels weird. "Sometimes, I nap, read two sentences, and then have to close my eyes again."

"This is just a warning letter, you haven't been put on academic probation yet. It's meant to encourage you to do better next semester. You don't have to worry about it. No one can tell you that you can't study."

I breathe through my frustration with her. As much as she

understands my predicament, she doesn't understand what's happening in my head. *I'm too stupid, and the university is embarrassed of me.*

"I don't want to talk about it anymore. Can you go, please?" I say to her as I crawl up on my bed and hug the closest pillow. "Wait," I say before she closes the door on her way out. I try to lift my head so I'm not mumbling into the pillow. "Can you cancel my day with Dad and James? I don't want to go anywhere."

"Of course." She responds sweetly and closes the door lightly. Usually, she slams doors shut as if she forgets there's a knob you can turn.

I listen as she immediately heads to James's door to tell him. I don't bother straining to listen to what she says to him. I don't need to hear someone explain how I'm an utter disappointment to society. I'm so stupid. I keep repeating it to myself. *I'm so stupid, I'm so stupid, I'm so stupid.* I know I shouldn't be saying this to myself. Growing up, Mom always had a rule that we couldn't call ourselves or anyone else stupid, and there's a reason. Calling someone stupid is hurtful; calling yourself stupid is even more so. And unrealistic. Calling anyone stupid is stupid because there's a broad spectrum of intelligence. Just because someone might not be book smart doesn't mean they're not clever.

I know Mom gets this from working with people with severe mental disabilities. She experiences firsthand people who can't be independent because they can't properly care for themselves in a society not built for them. Mom also sees those same individuals outsmart her without her realizing it. She always tells me how incredible clients can be with math or information recall. If she's looking to get updated on what is happening in the world, she can just go to someone, and they tell her exactly what they read in the paper, word for word. There are different types of intelligence. If it's not to do well in standardized schooling, I wonder what mine is.

I sit up and wipe my tears away. Although I love and respect anybody going through hard times, this isn't about anyone but myself. I feel like I'm fighting against society's expectations of how I should be. It doesn't matter what the fuck society thinks. If life isn't constructed for you, that doesn't mean you don't fit in it or don't deserve to live. Society is the wrong one. Humans are complex, and I think we've evolved enough to understand that at this point, or at least we should have.

As I'm going on with my internal debate, tears still on my pillow, Dad arrives to pick us up. I can hear Mom mumbling through the walls while she tells him I want to spend the day at home. I asked her not to tell Dad about the letter until I've conquered this. He's protesting, asking to come to my room. I shake my head, whispering the answer to him, hoping it goes well. As I make out Mom denying his request, things escalate, and I can hear James coming down the hall and stairs toward them. My self-pity is interrupted enough to break into a feeling of dread.

I didn't mean to be so much of a problem. I didn't mean for Dad to get hurt by my refusal. I just can't; I can't do anything. I shrink back into my bed puddle. Become one with comfort; maybe that will help. It doesn't, of course, but it puts me somewhere. I need to get back to my internal debate. Usually, I'm pretty good at reasoning things out; it's just that now, I need some extra time to get there, like with my schoolwork. That I failed in. Because it wasn't enough, but it was enough! *I swear to God, I passed those courses. How can they not think I'm good enough? This situation is stupid.* Mom interrupts my thoughts by opening the door to confirm that Dad's left and I don't have to worry about doing anything today. James has also decided to stay home.

"He wasn't happy about it, but things change, plans change, and you get over it. So he just left instead and went back to your uncle's." On a dime, she changes her attitude and asks, "What can I do for you? Can I make you something?"

Poor Dad, I know how awful it is for plans to change, trust me, and unlike Mom, I don't think he should just get over it. Unfortunately, that's not a thing.

"No..." I say to her. I think I may have been onto something.

"What about fresh cookies?"

This gets my attention. "With milk?"

"Sure!"

"Okay," I say to her, although, all I do is melt back into my puddle.

After she leaves again, shutting the door behind her, I take a minute to remember where I was in my thoughts. Stupid, notes, stupid, work, not like everyone else, fuck everyone else, into a puddle, disappointment in myself... *Oh, there it is.*

The world expects a certain level of intelligence from you. Whether you pass the classes or not, there's still an invisible level they expect you to achieve so they can take you seriously. I have already decided to try taking an extra course next semester. I need to get a math course for some reason, and I need to do it before I forget how to do the math. I made it through high school, taking the most challenging math courses. You can use a calculator now anyways. But understanding fundamentals is essential, and ultimately, finding an answer can be a way of thinking. Maybe I just suck at psychology and biology? My best marks by far were in anthropology, but is that because it was easier? No, I know some people in that course that weren't doing as well. Some even failed it.

Taking an extra course doesn't sound like such a good idea anymore. Where in society or the world do I fit in again? Oh yeah, fuck that, that's where. Fuck the world, and fuck where I'm *supposed* to be. This is where I am. I only need to worry about myself. I'm entering a land where I'm swearing to unlikeable amounts. I use it to give expression to my frustration, even if only in my head. If the rest of the world isn't going to consider me as whole, then I am responsible for doing it. I'll figure this out like I figured out how to reschedule my therapies to give myself the time I needed. My goal is to finish university and graduate with a degree. I don't know what I'll do for a job after that. That's a later problem.

Mom pops in to tell me the cookies are ready. I tell her I'm still not hungry, but the smell of the cookies has, at least, made me feel better. It adds to the warmth of my bed. I quickly bring myself back to my thoughts. *I have to pass my classes and graduate.* I mean, obviously, there are other things too: maintaining connections with family and friends, improving my physical abilities, and more.

* * *

My meeting with the psychologist is as I expect, seemingly unnecessary. I don't feel like I have time right now to focus on my mental health when so much of my physical health and education is consuming my life. I explain my schedule to her and the alterations I've made to make it more feasible. I tell her everything I can remember about my current life—it's a lot to fit into a short conversation. I vow to reciprocate someday the kindness shown to me somehow, but I need to work on myself first. If I can improve myself, then maybe someday I can be there for others like they are there for me. After just a few visits with her, we agree that my attention is best kept on my studies. An additional weekly appointment to add to my busy schedule won't help much.

Just live and breathe. Can that even happen? Well, we're about to find out. I still have therapy, of course. Frankly, I don't think I could live without my physical or massage therapy. My body hurts so much all the time, but at least I enjoy those more. I'm officially free of occupational therapy, and since I decided not to get any tutors for my new classes, I'm now free to study on my own. I'll go to physiotherapy and massage therapy once or twice a month each and then just study. Oh God, I need this time to study. It doesn't take long to realize the extra course was a bad idea, even with fewer appointments, but if I hang in there maybe I can just get through it for this one semester. Then, I'll settle on three courses at my regular pace.

Things don't work out with Matt, for many reasons, including the fact that my life is so consumed with my rehab and education. I try dating here and there, but I don't even know if dating is essential right now. Maybe I should just focus on my studies and graduate first. Still, you can't ignore the feeling you get when someone cares for you, even though they're not obligated to, as if you are chosen. It's an elation of feelings. These are the words of a young woman looking for more meaning to her life than therapy. *People often hide in relationships, so why should I be any different?* Regardless, having someone to hide behind is not the only thing I want from a relationship, and so with dating turning out to be more complicated than I hoped, I have to set the idea aside and continue working on myself instead.

Into my second semester, I walk into my anthropology class and realize I feel like I belong in this room, like I've found my comfort zone, the epitome of me. My first semester anthropology class focused mainly on cultural anthropology and the world's vast diversity. There are human civilizations almost no one knows anything about, and the class taught us how to learn from this. It was eye-opening. This semester, my anthropology class is delving deeper into that same topic. I love reading about different styles of living from my own. Living differently from the norm is irrelevant. I'm not so sure there is a *normal* anymore. If you look at the world and humanity, it would be virtually impossible to define a preferred way of living, or what people could collectively call *normal*. It's bullshit. There is no such thing.

In my new anthropology classes, the field of study opens avenues for me. I'm learning more about the world. There isn't only cultural anthropology but five leading schools from which humans can learn—cultural, physical, linguistic, forensic, and archaeological anthropology all build up our knowledge of humanity. I'm sure there's more if I want to go deep enough. I look forward to learning more about physical anthropology and archaeology in this class. The readings and lectures contain a beautiful combination of humanities and physical science. Science has always been a strong suit for me, mainly because I'm naturally a science girl. I like facts and puzzles. I also love math. 1+1=2. Simple. Indisputable. Easy to mark.

Or so I thought. Looking down at my math exam later in the semester, covered in red marks, I approach the professor to ask for an explanation.

"You didn't have the work right," she says.

"Are the answers correct?" I ask.

"Yes, but the whole point is to learn new methods of finding the answer, which you didn't do."

You have got to be kidding me. I'm always learning different techniques to find the same answer. This means I'll have to put more focus than I was expecting into this class.

From what I have learned in biology, math comes mainly from the brain's right side, and that's the side my injury affected most. The blood pooled in the centre, yes, but more heavily on the right—it explains why I was paralyzed on the left side of my body. Each side of the brain controls its opposite side of the body's motor capabilities, like a crisscross action. I can't escape the feeling that I will no longer be good at math. I'm just barely passing the course. If I can manage it and maybe do a summer course before I start work, I can have eight courses under my belt in the first year instead of the ten considered normal for students—just two less and that much closer to finishing.

I just barely pass all my second-semester courses, so I decide to stick to just one for the summer semester: Forensic Anthropology and Archaeology Field Study. It's a chance to learn more about anthropology while getting an additional credit. We learn about bone anatomy, what you can analyse about people by studying their bones, and different careers you can pursue using this knowledge. I learn a lot about myself in the lab with human bone models all around me. Next, we learn about archaeology in the field. I pass this summer course with flying colours and better grades than in any other class I took all year. It feels good to know I'm at least good at *something*.

But not everything. Mom and I go to Vancouver to visit James at school and celebrate that I made it through my first full year of university. It's nice to see where James lives. Staying on campus, in a hotel set aside for visiting family, flashbacks to my visit with Dad hit my heart. I haven't talked much to him since the incident. On a day we are supposed to tour Vancouver, I receive an email confirming my grades haven't gone up enough, and so the university is officially putting me on academic probation. Tears form in my eyes as I remind myself I've already been through this. When I return home, I can defend myself and get them to reverse it. But it still hurts, knowing I haven't lived up to the norm. *Oh yeah, fuck the norm.* That's what I'm supposed to be saying, right? I didn't go through all this personal growth just to have someone make me feel like I'm not good enough. In truth, I'm the one making myself feel like I'm not good enough, but either way, I know I deserve to be in university right now. I can't let this ruin my day like last time. I want to explore Vancouver without life getting in the way.

On our return, Mom says that now that my school year is up, she's ready to tell me that Dad's been emailing her regularly to see how I'm doing and wants to apologize. He wants to get back in touch. I feel better knowing that he didn't forget about me. I miss his regular calls. They're important.

Whether he knows and understands what I'm going through is more my problem than his. As soon as Mom tells me about his emails, I write to Dad and express that it will be easier for me to explain through text than over the phone. He agrees and tells me he understands; he's not upset with me.

In fact, now that we're emailing, he finds it easier to let me know that he's also been going through a hard time lately. He and my stepmom have decided to get a divorce. A second divorce can hit you in a way he didn't think possible. I respond, telling him my thoughts about change and how change can be hard sometimes. After this, our weekly calls start again, and I feel more comfortable. I hated the idea that I might not have had a relationship with him moving forward.

* * *

Back at The Toy Factory for the summer, I smile as I start to update inventory, still thinking about how I managed to finish my first year of university.

"Here's another box!" My boss, Bill, comes in and plops another box onto my pile. "Next, we'll have to inventory the wooden toys. We hired someone new this year, and I hope they'll do well in the workshop." Soon after I left the hospital, I had called Bill and confirmed to him that because of my circumstances, I wouldn't be able to work any of the saws or big sanding machines anymore. It saddens me to give up what I enjoyed most about working here, but I understand it. I can barely walk these days without hurting myself. I shouldn't be by any big machines. He continues, "It's too bad you can't make toys anymore. You were so good at it! If you change your mind, you can always let me know. I wouldn't mind training you again." I frown to myself, because I know the truth.

"No," I say with a frown. "I don't think that would be a good idea. My mom would have a heart attack if she learned I was making toys again." I laughed. It's easy to blame things on her, and thankfully, she and I have an agreement that I can do this whenever I want because it helps me feel more normal. "I'm sorry I'm taking away one of your toymakers, and now you have to train someone new. I think I could still assemble toys if you need an extra person, I just don't think I can use any big machines."

"We can work with that. It's always helpful to have someone assemble the toys. We could have someone cutting and you glueing and hammering."

I love the idea and tell him so. The idea that I could still help and do what I love while not being a risk is the best thing I could ask for. I mostly work in the store, interacting with customers and working the register. I even stock shelves, as long as it's not too heavy or high. My employers are great at not asking too much of me, but they allow me to do as much as I am comfortable with. They know the results of my work assessment and always keep that in mind.

Back at home, with everything still on my mind, I step out my front door onto the concrete veranda and take in the scenery I grew up around. Fresh air instantly hits my lungs and my mind finally shuts up. I take a deep breath, in and out, and sit on the front step. I rest my head on the beam beside me, doing my best to soak up the sun's warmth in this spot before it moves and casts a shadow in the front of the house. *This. This right here. This is why I came back home.* I know it's not actually the reason I came back home, but for a moment, it's effortless to believe this was the only reason. Charlottetown is beautiful, and if I were a city person, I would love it, as many others do. But here is where I belong.

I don't believe many places are so beautiful that they will literally shut me up, stop my thoughts on sight, and calm me. This is love.

I'm realizing more and more the amount of pain that exists in this world. The difficulties I'm having in my own life don't compare to the people who lack the amount of love, support, and privilege I have. I hope they all have a place like this, or a person or maybe even an object they can love so dearly it can quiet their problems. It's not only those in great distress either; everyone has problems. Everyone. I genuinely believe that. Because everyone has their own life with a complex history of physical, social, and emotional issues. Yes, some are inarguably worse than others. Humanitarian issues, such as food and water scarcity, should always be our top priority, and I'll never understand why they're not. Unfortunately, as a society, our top priorities are typically rooted in capitalism—our jobs, paycheques, and belongings.

As individuals and living beings, our top priority is naturally having shelter, food, and water. Shouldn't that be our primary goal when helping others? Yet when I hear stories of people lacking these necessities, and how some others don't want to be generous because they're worried about being taken advantage of, I wonder if I'll ever understand that thought process. Humans are pack creatures; we survive by being able to rely on each other. That's what I believe a community is. This person keeps our streets clean, this one takes care of our children, these people teach, and these take care of finances. It's a community, a hive; everyone has a role to play, and that's how we thrive as a species. (That, and thumbs, undoubtedly.) If someone is lagging behind, we need to be able to help them get back on their feet, not shun them. Even bees understand this.

I growl at myself for starting my mind up again and stop to look at the grass, a dark, rich green that I love so much. I reach out and feel the sharp blades dance on the surface of my palm until it reaches a dandelion, a soft and furry break from the light scratches. It's so buttery that I have to casually look at my hand to see if it leaves any bright yellow residue. It doesn't. But it leaves something; I'm just not sure what. A sensation. A feeling of wonder, a drive to protect this innocent, fragile flower. It's so small in its community of nature and photosynthesis. This is life at its finest and most authentic.

I look up. A vast display of green fields and trees of all colours come to my eyes, with a stripe of bright, sparkling water that separates two parts of the land. It's just a simple flower in a great, big world of possibilities and adventure. This flower remains in its spot, happy to soak in the sunshine because it can't really do anything else. It doesn't know any different. Humans can aspire to more; we can walk, talk, and pick things up. But I hope we can take a moment occasionally to remember who we are and where we come from. We're still a part of nature and need everything that nature requires. We need sunshine; fresh air; a healthy, supportive societal system; and, of course, time to rest. My brain injury might not have automatically given me insight into people's minds—I will have to learn how to do that better myself—but it has magnified the fundamentals of living and what I need or can let go.

Chapter Eight: Anthropology

I am incredibly thankful for my summer reset before returning to classes in September. That mess with the academic probation was even easier to settle than I had hoped. I only had to send one email about it and I was told I could continue my classes like normal. This year will now give me an idea of what to expect for the rest of my university years. I'm going into my third year of recovery, living at home with Mom driving me in to UPEI on her way to work. I could only afford to pay rent for the first year of university, a fact I knew from the very beginning. Kristy, Loriann, and I had only ever just wanted to experience what living on our own would be like. I'll now have no choice but to stay in Charlottetown while Mom finishes her workday.

She surprised me this past summer with the most wonderful present on my birthday: tickets to see Elton John in his *Greatest Hits* concert in Summerside this fall. I can't believe he is coming to this tiny Island! Someone so big and famous, such an enormous help in my life, is coming here to sing my favourite songs. *And I get to attend?!* Thinking about everything I've been through in the past couple of years, I can't help but feel like this is fate. I imagine addressing him, humbly letting him know of my gratitude as though he's some kind of deity. *Elton John, dear Sir John. I swear you must have known that I needed this. Somehow, you ensured I could get these tickets through the people at the Credit Union Place. Same as you knew I would find your album when I was feeling distressed trying to learn how to study anew. Thank you.* I mean, I don't believe in any higher beings, but I don't know how else to speak to someone who isn't here. I'm not yet sure if I'd consider myself an atheist because it sure is nice to be able to look up sometimes and be thankful or maybe even ask for help when you need it. My religious beliefs will remain an adventure I've yet to explore. *The concert will be on September 14th, and it's not far away!*

I watch the vibrant trees and grass pass me on the way to school. My classes will be interesting in the second year. I'll be deciding on my major this year. Previously I wanted to major in psychology, but I found one of my classes last year brought up unexpected past trauma. When I was in class, I listened to my professor tell me the basics of psychiatry. Without bringing up an image of the brain, she discussed how the brains of some individuals aren't like others, and how we are able to study this and map out their complications. I left class that day crying.

Even the best scholars don't know enough about the brain. It hurts me to be reminded that not enough research has been put into the brain to truly understand it, and so even psychologists and psychiatrists cannot tell you what you can expect from any outcome. *Do I really want to spend the next three years learning something that might bring up such memories and feelings of hurt? To be reminded of how my brain works, how it compares to others, and how society technically considers me 'abnormal' now? I think not.* And so, I eliminated psychology from my options for a major. Biology was the worst of the four classes I took last year. It was too much memorization, and my poor brain couldn't handle it. I'm smart. I believe this, but I'm not sure that's the way to go when memorization is a weakness for me right now. I need something that fits me better.

That leaves anthropology. I'm enjoying how the field embraces learning and looks at every human society through its individual structure. Of course, with respect, it's not perfect, but its fundamentals are what I love. The field recognizes every group of people as unique—with their own unique social groupings, histories, and economic or environmental influences. People should do this with the brain, and I often wonder why they don't. I think it's because people try and relate it too much with things they already know. They want to feel like they know everything about themselves. I can get that. But admitting what you don't know can help you develop.

I'm starting with Cultural Anthropology, Introduction to Archaeology, and Introduction to Greek. Each of these courses will help me grasp a different subfield of anthropology, with Introduction to Greek covering ancient Greek text and representing early linguistics.

In my classes, I look around to see if I can befriend any more anthropology lovers; however, because I'm still technically taking introductory courses, most of the faces around me look fresh out of high school. They look young and like they don't know what to expect from university yet.

My first couple of weeks fly by, and before I know it the weekend of the Elton John concert is here. I can't contain my excitement. My body quietly shakes the whole drive to Summerside, and I can only imagine how annoying my happiness must be, with me moving so much in my seat and rambling on. Still, I hope it's refreshing. This, here, is a night we both deserve. Mom has been incredibly supportive, holding my hand while I walk at a snail's pace, getting me anything I need, and of course she's been a shoulder to cry on. I give her a quick glance. I know she needs this night as much as I do.

"Are you excited?!" I ask her for probably the tenth time.

"It sure is nice to get out," she responds with only a sprinkle of excitement in her voice, unlike the waterfall in mine. She perks herself up. "How about you? You've done nothing but talk about Elton John this past year, and now he'll be in Summerside. Can you believe it?"

"No," I laugh. "But do you even know any of the songs he'll be playing tonight?"

"Of course I do. These are his greatest hits. I grew up with this music. I'm just astonished that you like it so much."

"Me too. But sorry," I shrug dramatically. "I can't explain it. It just works for me. My taste in music doesn't usually stay the same, though. Still, I'll always remember that with his music, I found the study groove I needed to pass my courses last year. Even if I find a new artist to play while studying, that first year was so important that I'll never forget it. I won't forget this album, his voice, and I love him so much!"

"Really? Are you saying he's your celebrity crush?" My mom glances at me.

"Oh. No, that's not what I mean. I've been busy keeping my grades up enough to pass my courses. I don't know everything about his life, Mom! I don't have the time to be into celebrity news like that. I may have had celebrity crushes when I was younger, but not now."

Pulling up to the Credit Union Place in Summerside, this event feels like the biggest the Island has ever hosted. As we tried to manoeuvre through the heavy traffic, we aim to get a parking spot near the entrance so I can stay energized before the concert starts. It's already hours longer than most things I've tried attending since the brain injury. It'll be a tiring but wonderful night, and then I'll have the weekend to rest before classes on Tuesday. It's so worth it!

Our seats are much closer to the front than I expected, and while we wait, Mom asks if there's a particular song that I'm hoping he sings tonight. I nod to her and answer, but the place is too loud and crowded for her to hear. No matter, though, the concert soon begins. When "Your Song" (or as I like to call it, *my* song) comes on, I get her attention to tell her this is it, mouthing *this* and emphatically pointing my finger at the stage until she nods.

* * *

With a tremendous start to the school year, I can feel nothing but optimism for what's to come, fogged only a little by hesitation from experience. I decide to go and get my second tattoo. I owe it to myself to have something that will epitomize my accident and the lifetime fight for myself it's put me in. So, I pick my two favourite words I've ever heard next to each other: *forget regret*.

You need to forget what you wish you could've done in life. Moving forward, I only focus on today and what's vital for me for the future. Where do I want to be in life? How will I get there with what I have? Beyond that, I don't want to make choices I know I'll regret later. I do just that when I choose to get up every day since the accident. I do it because I know if I don't, I'll regret it. This belief is what's gotten me this far, and it's how I choose to live going forward. I'll live by making choices I won't regret and focusing on what's best for me and everyone around me. I'm exaggerating the line, but isn't that what you should do? Be open to interpretation, look at things through your own lens, and enjoy it for all it is and could be. This phrase allows you to do that.

Walking out of my bedroom to get a snack, the fresh tattoo still hot on my arm, Mom gives me a look.

"How are you feeling? Sore?" She asks me as I approach her, a smug smirk on her face. I laugh at her.

"It's a bit sore, but not that bad. Trust me, nothing is as sore as the shit I had to deal with in the hospital. Remember that needle they used to give me almost every day after I came back to the island? The one in my stomach?"

"No… which one are you talking about? I remember when they took blood out of a vein in your wrist and watched your face twist while it was happening. The left side of your face was still a little frozen. You didn't move it that much back then, but it moved when you were in pain. I remember that."

"Oh yeah. I remember that, too. It must have been later in the summer for me to remember it." I frown. "That sucked. The nurses couldn't find a vein in my arm like a normal person."

"Yeah, because you have deep, slippery veins, like me!"

"Thank you for that," I sarcastically say as I smile sweetly at her.

"You're welcome," she says in the same sweet tone. She quickly adds, "Hey, I got them from your grandfather, so you can blame him!"

"Yeah, but he's not here to complain to." I get back to what I was saying. "No! I'm talking about the one they'd give me in my stomach. I think it was for blood circulation? Man, that hurt like…" I pause, moving my teeth from my lips to stop myself from saying, the F word. I can curse in my head when I need it, but I'm not sure I'm ready to swear in front of my mother, so if I could learn to keep it inside, that'd be great.

"Oh yeah, I think I remember that one. I think you usually got it in the middle of the day or in the morning when I wasn't there. Maybe that's why I didn't think of it. But you needed to get that! You weren't moving much, and something had to keep your blood pumping so you could heal." She gave me a gentle nudge.

"Anyway," I casually push her away and get up. *That's not the point.* "Trust me, after getting that burning injection almost every day, the pain of a small tattoo is nothing. That needle felt like they were inserting literal fire into my stomach. And now, at least, I've got something to show for the pain I've gone through. Something that proves I experienced and withstood it."

"You're walking again! I think that proves it just fine!"

"Yeah, but even though walking is still a bit of a struggle for me, I've improved so much that I notice it's hard for others to remember. Like, I'm just normal and don't have a reason for being this tired. I don't know. It's hard to explain." Done with the conversation, I head to the kitchen for a snack. But Mom follows me.

"I know you don't remember much from right after your accident, but do you remember much else from being at QEH? I've always been curious to see if you remembered doing the things you did in the hospital. Most days when you were there, you couldn't even remember what happened the day before."

"I remember some things." I open the fridge, moving one hand while I talk. "Like the needle. I remember a couple of the rooms I was in, what the beds felt like, that shake you used to make me with the chocolate milk. I remember the taste of it."

"That was chocolate milk and protein powder your brother picked for you. You needed extra protein to build back your bones and muscles."

"Yeah, that was delicious! I remember it tasting like the best thing in the world!"

"I can get it for you again if you'd like. You can try it and see if it still tastes that good or if you were just so deprived of flavour from eating nothing but hospital food." She laughs.

"Yeah! Let's do that! But you have to get the chocolate milk too."

"Okay, I'll do that."

"Anyway, back to your question. Yeah, I remember stuff in general and some small details. Still, I can't play out a whole day or anything, not by myself anyway. I also only have select memories, but there's a lot I don't remember. While I don't remember anything from the first hospital, I still refuse to read that notebook you said you wrote for me. Not much from the second hospital is super clear either. It feels like so long ago." I close the fridge, realizing I didn't see a thing while it was open, and turn to her to continue. "You've told me many stories, though, of when I was in the hospital, so usually, most of my memories are a weird mix of the stories you told me and some small things I remember. Oh, and I also add flair to it. For example, when you mention a person in your stories, I can't say I remember them. But, if I know them, I'll add in what I'd imagine their behaviour to be like. There's no real way of telling if those memories are made up or real."

Mom ponders this for a second. "That's very interesting. You were pretty foggy a lot of the time, so you're right. There's no way of knowing."

I shrug. *That's my reality.* Now I've got to focus on schoolwork. I take my glass, deciding it's enough to hold me for now. This walk to the kitchen was more of a study break than a snack break, so I return to my room.

I pause, briefly drawn in by the TV like a moth to a flame for a moment, and Mom, who has found her way back to her seat, turns to me again and says, "I think your story would make a good book someday. You could inspire others to make it through as you have."

"Are you freaking kidding me?" I say in the nicest way possible. "Nobody wants to hear my depressing story! I don't even want to hear it. If only I could forget all about it and forget that pain and struggle. God, no. No, no, no, no. And writing it? It'd be like going through it all over again! I can't do that to myself. That's a horrible idea."

Mom squirms a little. "Alright, well, maybe you're not ready to write a book about it yet, but someday you might be. In that case, you should write down everything you remember. Then, you can use that along with the book I wrote for you in Moncton. I can't remember if I wrote anything about your time at QEH, so you might only have those weird memories of yours to work with."

"Trust me, that's stuff I'll never forget. It's stuck in there like freaking glue." I tap my head as I turn away from her ridiculous idea toward my room and present reality.

* * *

Most of my classes are in the morning. Mom starts picking me up on her lunch break to take me to my Aunt Amelia's house for the afternoons, so studying midday is quieter. I come here almost daily now, even when I come to town just for a therapy appointment—I still have many of those. I stay on campus when I have an extra thing or two I need to do there or when it works out better for Mom's schedule. I only stay home if I have no classes or appointments so I can study and nap in my bed. It doesn't happen often, but those days are special.

On campus, you can find me in a large lounge nearest most of my classes. At Aunt Amelia's, you'll find me on the couch in the company of her two Saint Bernards, who are either at my feet or by the window watching squirrels. They bark at a leaf outside now and then, but for the most part, I have them trained like I do Lindor and Littlefoot—to lay down and keep calm and quiet so I don't get too distracted from my schoolwork. It's excellent having dogs as study buddies. One second, I can be stuck while writing a sentence, frozen because I can't think of the right word, and the next, I feel a heavy, warm head gently placed on my lap because this pupper has decided to be the centre of my universe. Ignoring images of the hospital that pop into my head, I stop to pet the dog. *Fine, I will get up off my stiff ass and go to the door for a breath of fresh air.*

I direct my thoughts to Aunt Amelia and her family as I do this. We got close when we volunteered together with the Canadian Red Cross. Even though Mom and I are no longer volunteers, our connections there have lasted. Mom calls to tell me that one of the couples we met there, friends Donna and Stan, have invited us to their house this weekend. Unfortunately, Stan was diagnosed with a severe form of cancer a year or two ago. I'm not sure when the diagnosis happened, to be honest. I think I was too caught up in my own therapy to ask or remember, but now I tell her I want to be more involved.

So far, from what I hear, Stan's cancer is progressing quickly, he pretty much doesn't leave the house, and he's having a hard time moving around. Mom's been supporting Donna as a fellow caregiver, making me feel that it's my job to do the same for Stan as a fellow patient. He now has to live his life dependent on others, realizing things will never be the same again. So far, all I've done for him is lend him my old orange cane, but sitting down and talking with him would be nice. I tell Mom I'm very excited to be able to see them. I hang up the phone and get ready to nap before my cousins get home.

On the drive to visit Stan and Donna, Mom reminds me that Aunt Amelia has been working on a surprise project for Stan. He doesn't have much on his bucket list. He's already done most things, but one of his most significant wishes is to make an impact on the world. The last time we visited, he told us about the butterfly effect. He told us he wanted to be like a butterfly's wing that flutters, pushes the wind, and makes an effect that could one day change the world. He said it doesn't have to change the whole world, and that even if he could have an effect on an individual he would feel complete. Being there at the time, my entire family tried to convince him he had that kind of effect on people every day, but we knew that we didn't convince him.

Aunt Amelia's project is to create a book made up of Stan's Facebook posts. He makes one every day, updating people on his recovery and outlook on life. They're all messages of inspiration and love of life. It's a gift to prove to him that he's been impactful in his everyday life. Mom tells me that today's the day we're presenting this book to him.

We each wrote a separate piece for it, plus an introduction and a note to Stan. My contribution is a poem because I like poetry so much. It shares how wonderful it is to have met Stan. I want him to know that he's the kind of person someone can befriend easily. He makes people feel comfortable, and that alone is admirable. I open the book to read through my poem before presenting it to him.

A Connection So Deep

That you can feel safe
That you can immediately be yourself
That you will always have memories to keep.
It is something you do not take advantage of
Someone to learn from and make you want to be a better person
Something to love, a connection so deep.
I'll love and cherish you forever.
—*Sweetie Kamya* (because he often calls me sweetie)

When we arrive, we give our hugs to Donna and settle in the living room around Stan and the chair he sits in most days. I hug this man who sits with my orange cane resting on the back of his chair. He's about a quarter of the size he was when I first met him. Still, I'll never forget him as the jolly man with a belly with whom I have good conversations while Mom, my aunt, and Donna are chatting. I guess this is why the two of us have always been closer. I often gravitate to the husbands of Mom's friends because it's impossible to get a word in otherwise. Stan and I always had fun chats together. I won't get him all to myself today because he's the centre of attention. Still, all these memories wash over me as I hug his stick-figure body before finding my seat across the room. I have a moment before everyone settles and the chatter starts.

I smile and ask him, "How do you like the cane?" I'm sincerely happy he let me lend it to him instead of renting one for himself.

"It's working great! I love the funky colour. It spices up my life," he says with a soft chuckle.

"Yeah, it's important not to lean into the boring. That can swallow you up. I chose a bright colour to help get me out of that life of being unable to go anywhere or do anything..."

I feel myself getting way too personal too fast, making things awkward. While the cane eventually brought me out of my pitiful funk, he has no way of escaping his. Mom rescues me immediately, and the women start up, their chatter so loud that Stan and I can no longer chat. Because Stan can only withstand short visits, we bring out the book pretty soon and present to him.

When it's time for us to leave, I wait to say goodbye to Stan last so that maybe we can exchange a few more words to make up for the awkwardness earlier.

"Thank you for the book," Stan says as he gives me a tighter hug with more strength than before. "I love your poem. It means so much to me. I hope you know I look to you and everything you've done and gone through as inspiration. Your cane reminds me daily that I can keep moving forward as you did."

"Oh my God. That means the world to me. But I hope you know that this," I tap on the book on his lap. "This is real. You're a wonderful person, and you have wonderful things to say. I'm so glad we could put it together in a book for you."

"Oh, thank you so much, sweetie." He gives me another hug. "Maybe you'll write a book too someday."

I give him a little hug, while mumbling about how I'd consider it, knowing full and well that the opinion I gave Mom still stands. My life is too much of a jumble right now to really think about it.

* * *

Stretching my legs, I balance myself on the rug to avoid the cold concrete where Mom set up my treadmill, a TV, and a couch for me. Deciding I'm not getting a deep enough stretch sitting on the floor, I stand up and move to the treadmill. Using its arm to steady myself, I attempt a few of the positions Lisa showed me at physio. With both hands on the arm and one leg on the treadmill, I lean forward while bending my back leg to get a stretch in my calf. It's still tight and is probably the reason my foot keeps dropping. I've been doing this stretch for over two years now.

I didn't do it yesterday, though, and it's fucking showing. I push myself away from the treadmill. Nobody is home, so I let out a loud groan, nearly a scream. My eyes tear up in frustration. *It just won't stretch!* I give the treadmill a very light kick. I know that if I waste time crying over this stupid little detail that's been bugging me for years now, it'll just advance into more extensive issues. I'll never get on the treadmill, practise walking, shower for the day, and return to studying. So, I blink the tears away with anger at myself, the world, life and its hardships, then decided I tried anyway, and that's what matters.

I hop on the treadmill, trying to focus my thoughts on my music instead of myself. Walking at a nice, slow pace so as not to hurt myself, the song "Temporary Home" by Carrie Underwood comes on. It's a beautiful piece of music filled with multiple short stories of people who believe everything in life is only temporary. If life isn't what you want it to be now, you always have something to look forward to. Or at least, that's how I usually understand it. I originally put it in my playlist in case it might come on in a moment like this when I hate my life and think everything is horrible and sucks. I remember wanting it to act as a beacon of hope. I'm having one of those times now; time to test this baby out. I focus on the lyrics while ensuring my feet move correctly.

All I hear is its beginning, and suddenly, my thoughts are no longer on myself, but on the lyrics to the song.

They remind me of how complex individuals can be, and how most people don't like to recognize this. I stop the treadmill when my ten minutes are up. It's a little less than I hoped to do today, but my mind is whirling with these thoughts. I think to myself about how unfortunate the world is to be like this, so black and white. *Be the change you want to see in the world.* It's a familiar quote that comes to mind now. I stretch forward to see if my calf has become looser from the walk. It has, but only by a small fraction. Just because this is how life is doesn't mean this is how it's always going to be.

* * *

Over the rest of the second semester, I focus on my classes: Greek Art, the Evolution of Human Culture, and learning about the Aboriginal Peoples of Canada, all while dating a little and making new friends. I finish the school year certain that anthropology is where I thrive. My choice of a major is proven right after I complete another Forensic Anthropology and Archaeology Field Methods course at a higher level, with my highest grade yet: eighty-eight percent. That's a much more comfortable grade than the fifties I earned in my first year. The relief I feel is inexplicable. Maybe I *am* good enough. A weight has lifted a little more with the knowledge that I'm studying something I love and am good at. I have no idea what I'll do with it after I graduate, but right now, I just need to be doing something I love, and if I can get a degree out of it, great.

Summer is peaceful and quiet. Most of my time is spent outside with the dogs and at work. My employers at The Toy Factory have helped me make a work schedule that works best for me, about sixteen to twenty-one hours a week. Sixteen hours works best; this allows me to have a little bit of a life outside of work and not be in too much physical pain from standing for hours. It's how I remember feeling before the accident when I could work full-time and still have the energy to do things outside work.

On the other hand, I've discovered that twenty-one hours feels like the equivalent of full-time plus additional hours before my brain injury. I still suffer through twenty-one-hour weeks here and there, though—I feel like I need to at least pull my weight with part-time hours. Brain injuries are all different, and I'm constantly finding where my limitations are.

For my twentieth birthday, I welcome Stan to join me for my celebrations by the water at our friends Ralph and Rachel's house, who are also friends we made at the Red Cross. It's expected this will be our last big party with Stan. His cancer is spreading faster and faster, so we make sure the day is as memorable as possible. We spend the day sitting by the water, watching the eagle's nest, and sharing fun stories while the BBQ lets off a sweet array of aromas and colours. Aunt Amelia made a butterfly cake for us, decorated yellow with a monarch in the middle. Looking over at Stan, I smile sweetly. *There's no other way I would have wanted to spend this birthday.*

I have a mediation scheduled for the end of the summer, to help assess what the outcome should be regarding the case between me and the car insurance companies. I'm still working with the insurance companies to arrive at a settlement that will help me with my expenses moving forward, in regard to my brain injury and the new kind of life that will come with it. Even after a previous mediation I still haven't received that settlement, and it seems to me that the lawyers are having a hard time concluding what I require for the future. I try not to judge them too harshly; I don't know what to expect either. On the drive to the lawyer's office, I look to Mom again for clarification.

"I'm sorry. I may have asked these questions before."

"No, don't apologize, Kamya. I'm happy to answer all your questions to the best of my ability."

"I remember the last mediation, but I prepared myself for the worst, and things became very anticlimactic. Nothing happened the way I expected it to. Not that I would've wanted anything bad, but I'm just hoping to know what to expect this time."

"First of all, that was something called a discovery—not a mediation—and that's what this one may be too, I don't know. I don't think we've done a mediation yet. In a discovery, the lawyers get together to assess what they know about you and your case. If they can't reach an agreement after that, they meet again with an impartial mediator in a mediation to help them reach an agreement. That's all I remember. I'm learning about this as we go, too. They'll ask questions, but your lawyer will prep you before we go in. He offered to meet with you earlier, but I told him right before it would be better because of your short-term memory."

"Thank you. I appreciate that."

"Other than that," she continues, "you probably know as much as I do. We're just going because your lawyer told me it'd be better if you were there. You've had a couple of neuropsych evaluations since the hospital. Maybe there's new information they need to go over with you. Also, you just had your last neuropsych exam a few months ago.

That marked three years since your accident when the doctors said we should expect your progress to plateau."

"Ugh. Those neuropsych exams take so much out of me," I say.

"You did your best."

"Thank God I never have to do that again, now that three years are up."

"That's not necessarily true."

"What? But I thought they were to measure my neuropsych abilities, and if the doctors say my progress will plateau after the first three years, then what's the point in doing it again? Or what, even, is the rush? If we really want to know where I stand mentally, which I don't care about, we can do it after I graduate, but still, why? Why would we do that?" Panic is in my voice, and I hope she hears it.

"Oh, I get it now." Mom shakes off my questions with understanding. "You're not doing those neuropsych evaluations just to see where you are with your progress. Yes, it's nice to know where you are in your brain's healing, but that's not why you're doing them. God, I'm not that cruel. I know how much of a toll they take on you."

"I don't think you do," I say slowly. "Well then, why am I doing them?"

"We're doing them for the insurance companies. We can't assume that the lawyers will take your word for how much help you need, so the tests prove your state professionally. I don't know if you'll need to do another one. But you're right. Now that the first three years after your brain injury are up, I can't imagine they'd see any change." Mom knows more than me, and she's looking at the big picture: me as an adult, not able to work full time, and possibly requiring regular, expensive therapy so that I can even dream to live a normal life.

"Oh." I blink and stare out the window. She must have told me this at some point, but I chose to believe it differently. I wonder why I'd do that to myself. Maybe because it was easier to comprehend? I ask, "Are we meeting with the lawyers representing the two insurance companies today?"

"Yes, Scott will be there, too, I think. He's the younger one working with your lawyer, Bill," she says.

"Oh, okay, I like Bill, and Scott's nice too, although I don't know him as much."

"You can talk to him when we get there, if you want."

I think about Bill and how I've come to trust him. I feel like I can tell him everything without holding back. Sometimes, when he asks a question, I hesitate and look at Mom, knowing I don't want to destroy her and make her think she isn't doing enough for me, and he'll say, "No, Kam. Don't worry about your mom, look at me and tell me. I need every detail if I'm going to help you."

The real thing starts after a quick chat with him in a boardroom. I am walking into a room full of lawyers sitting around what looks like a dining room table as if we're friends sharing a meal. For the life of me, I can't remember if I even said hi to Scott. *Too late now.* I take my seat, and the recorder announces the beginning of our meeting.

When the meeting is finished, I get out of the building and into the car as fast as my legs can take me and as fast as Mom can unlock the car doors. I get into the car, fuming. Unfortunately, the case is still not settled, and now I will surely have to do more tests. As Mom starts driving and the building is no longer in sight, I suddenly let loose.

"That was bullshit!"

Mom continues to focus on the road.

"I know," she says softly. "It's over now. You're fine. You did great. Even Bill said so. You just weren't there to hear it because you left so fast."

"I know. I had to get out of there. You just need to let me rant a little bit. It has been years, and they still don't believe me?"

"It's not that they don't believe you. They're just trying to ensure you aren't exploiting them. Until they reach an agreement, everything you do will be fair game. It might feel like your whole life is their business right now. That happens when you rely on others to give you enough money to help support you and your appointments for the rest of your life. These meetings help get to know you and determine the truth of your situation."

"Well, that won't work! Not many people besides you and me really know or see me having trouble because I hide it. I probably hide it too freaking well. And what were all those tests for if they won't take them seriously?" I put my hands over my eyes. I'm saying stuff I don't fully understand. It's so frustrating. "Fuck!" I finally yell out loud, and the resonance of it wakes me up. "Oh Shit. Sorry, Mom. I don't mean to swear in front of you."

"I don't care if you swear in front of me." She glances at me with the perfect *I don't give a fuck* kind of face and continues. "This was a really fucked up day, and you've been through a lot of fucked up shit. You can say fuck all you want. As long as I can say it too. Fuck!" I laugh at her. *Thank God.* Tension is released in my shoulders. I've slowly been discovering how much of a relief it is to just vocalize my frustration through curse words and the like. Not that I plan on cursing like this forever. Someday I hope to be able to find the words to express what I'm truly feeling, but until then, if the only way I can express my frustration is by using the F word, then I'm not going to judge myself for it.

"Deal." I smile, but I'm not done ranting yet, and she knows it. "I just can't do any more of this. It's bad enough trying to pass my classes. I don't want to get another one of those academic probation letters."

"I know, but at least you didn't show it in there. I thought you were doing perfectly fine before you burst out at me. It scared me, really."

I laughed and apologized for taking all my anger and frustration out on her. "You're right. I have nothing to hide. I'm no liar; there's fucking proof. Maybe they should just look at the doctor's and psychologist's notes. This is bullshit. Just take me home, please." And she does. I sit back. It's taking so much out of me to figure all of this out, and that's no one's fault but my own. It's my life, and my problem. All I want to do is direct the blame somewhere, but that would be unfair. Instead, I continue to try and hold it inside.

Back at home, I head straight to my room. Somehow, the emotions I experienced today have ignited a flame of frustration inside me with no way to be released. I close my door behind me and try to cry my feelings out, but my eyes are bone dry. It's too much. Can they break me to the point where I can't even cry? Is that possible? To get so upset and filled with troubles that tears won't come? I lie down and stare at the ceiling. I feel, yet again, like I need to pick up the pieces of my shattered life. Taking a shaky breath, I close my eyes and try to accept the unknown—again.

Chapter Nine: Diversity

Stepping on the treadmill, I press the start button. After I walk the starter pace for about a minute, I increase it slightly. This is a fast walk for me, and it's about as far as I'll push myself, but I feel ambitious. When I go any faster, it usually leads to a twisted ankle or overworked knee. Then, I spend many months trying to return to where I was before. I've already proved to myself that I can run, but I also established that I'm not quite ready for it consistently, and I may never be. If I stay at a slow pace, I have less chance of getting injured, so I'll slowly build myself up instead. It's not like I want to be weak and slow, but through painful trial and error over the last few years, I've learned that less is more, but a little is better than nothing. As I get more into the music, I decrease the speed again to focus on more than just my feet. "Raise a Little Hell" by Trooper plays at full volume. I love these lyrics.

My feet move, one by one, in front of each other. *I dig in my heels*; heel, toe; heel, toe. My focus is constantly on my feet, how they feel, how they move, and how they bring me forward. I look up, inspired by the music. *I'm fucking raising a little hell on my own, alright. I'm not letting the stress of this case screw up my progress.* I glance back down. *Shit,*

I think, as I notice my heels no longer hitting the treadmill pad first. *Ugh. I'm never going to get this right.* I'm stomping on my heels so much they are starting to feel tender. Now that the first three years of more significant progress are over, this could be a problem that will take years to fix, if I can fix it at all. At least the typical person walking next to me doesn't usually notice. As long as I take my regular scheduled naps, I don't trip over my feet so much. With some management, I can look just as clumsy as the average Joe or Nancy, which is something to be proud of. If only I could see that, but all I see is the mountain of things yet to be accomplished.

After my walk, I stretch for about twenty minutes before returning to my computer to study. This year, my new classes are Field Methods; Evolution of the Brain and Social Behaviour; and Myths of Love, Sex, and Marriage. As an online course, the latter allows me to spend more time at home studying and taking extra naps. Sometimes, I can pause a lecture halfway through. Myths of Love, Sex, and Marriage is a first-year religious studies course. We're learning about ancient myths and legends rooted in religion, how they've shaped the world, and about different religions and their similarities. With my mind wandering, I pause the lecture to research a few religions to distinguish them further, such as Judaism, Christianity, Catholicism, and Presbyterianism.

I guess my problem with religion is akin to my problem with psychology. I feel hostile towards both ideologies. There is way too much to infer and too many predispositions. I know there's a lot of study and research integrated into religion, but if God is omnipotent, then why didn't he see that we were about to be hit by another vehicle? Suppose God can guide us and lead us into making good decisions; why do most wars start over conflicting religious beliefs? If religion is a belief system, why do people care so much if people believe differently? Did God put me through this accident to teach me an important life lesson? If so, I can't say that it's fully appreciated.

And lastly, why, oh my God, why, does he let people who don't actually know me give him credit for all the hard work I put into my therapy? As if I wouldn't have gotten better otherwise? I was still in the hospital, fighting for the ability to walk and eat without choking, when I was reading messages online from people who sent their prayers and hopes. Among them, I'd read words like, "It's because of the Lord's work that she is alive and walking again. Thank the Lord!" *The Lord didn't fucking do shit; I did. I chose to get up every day. I put effort into raising my legs and improving my motor skills. It was me. Stop taking the credit away from me.* I think of this every time I remember that post. It makes me feel hateful, and I don't like it. I can feel myself getting angrier the longer I'm unable to express myself and describe what I'm going through. I can only hope that's something I manage to do for myself in the future. I remind myself that religion is believing, and to believe is to have hope. I have hope, so where does that put me?

Learning about religion through an anthropological lens helps. It doesn't matter what I do or don't believe because some people do. Hope and strength are powerful; I know that much. What I'll never understand is how people will judge and kill others who believe in something different. You can't force anyone to seek religious help. People should want it and feel the need for it themselves. So why is there this need for religions to be so exclusive? To hate anyone that doesn't subscribe to one's worldview? Religion is more than a belief. It's a connection with the people around you. When I was in the hospital, it was encouraging words and therapeutic help showing me the way, not a ray of sunshine. But you don't have to connect with everybody. I know many I'll never connect with.

Ignoring my thoughts on religion because I'm in no rush to see them through to a conclusion, I straighten my legs and look at them. I often study in improper positions on the couch by my treadmill. This is the room I spend most of my days in lately. From its crossed position, a shooting pain hits my right knee. It's from an injury I suffered from running on the stairs over a year ago now, and it still bothers me. I remind myself not to cross my legs for the millionth time because that makes it worse. I twisted my leg the wrong way once a long time ago, and now we focus on it every time I go to physio. Ultrasound, acupuncture, ice, and heat. And exercises; there are *always* more exercises to do. It's finally starting to feel like a normal knee, but I only need to sit in the wrong position for a moment, and the pain shoots again, making my knee feel weak. It radiates and pulses up and down, reminding me that I am delicate.

Humans are fragile creatures. There are muscles under muscles, keeping bones in place. It's impossible to imagine how significant each is until one stops working, putting added strain on the rest. And there's no great way to target those deep muscles to strengthen them while easing the stress on the ones around them; in time, though, they'll grow back. Some already have. Now though, it feels like it's taking forever. I have to stop myself from thinking that by the time I finally build back all of the muscles I lost from being paralyzed, I'll be old, and my pain will come from degeneration.

Finally, after finishing the lecture video, I can read a book for my other class. Captivating stories about human civilizations and alternative ways of living put me in a better mood. I look up at the clock to see how much of the day I have left to study and notice a part of the wall is black. I blink and blink again. Still black. Standing up carefully, I walk over to the wall to touch it. The blackness moves a little as I walk. Touching the black part of the wall, my hand disappears. I move my head, thinking it's just a shadow, and see no difference. I take a deep breath, fatigue hitting me in the gut, and instinctively glance at the room's focal point. The blackness moves with my eyes, covering the TV. Still holding onto the wall, I look all around the room to see if the blackness follows, and it does. I slowly walk back to the couch, holding onto things on my way. It's like my vision has halved.

Am I going blind? Can I be so tired that I'm going blind? What's happening?

I take my books, put them on the floor, and quickly decide that if I can't see my notes, I can't study. I might as well take a nap now. I'm calmer than I should be, but maybe that's because I am too tired to care. As I close my eyes, I start to ponder whether my fatigue could be causing this somehow. Maybe I am so tired that my brain has swelled, affecting my vision. Maybe my brain is playing tricks on me to force me to rest. *I did decide if I can't see my notes, I might as well take a break, so maybe? Could I be just imagining this to trick myself into resting?* Needing to stop my mind, I do my best to forget about it and drift off for a few hours. When I wake up, I can see my notes and the walls just fine, but I go upstairs to get a snack in case my blood sugar is low—another theory of mine. When I return, I aim to finish studying for the day so I can rest before bed.

* * *

It is not long before we get the news that our friend Stan passed away in palliative care. We visited him not long ago, so we had our last goodbyes without knowing they were our last. I had been planning to see him again; I wanted to colour a picture for him to put on the wall to brighten his room. I cry, thinking about how I should've done that for him sooner. I never got to put pictures up on his wall for him. I used to love the coloured pictures I had when I was in the hospital. It made the room look happier. It could have made his last days more manageable.

His funeral is full of people: fellow volunteer firefighters, family, community members, and fellow Red Cross volunteers. Everyone's mentioned in the eulogy he prepared because they all meant so much to him. Knowing an end was inevitable, he wrote a special goodbye to all of us, and they read it aloud for us all to hear. It's almost as if he is here, mourning with us. With everyone here with him, it's an appropriate way to celebrate his life. Standing by the gravesite is the hardest part for me. I don't know if it's just the end of a long day or the finality of him being gone. When facing the fact that I almost died, this is the feeling I feared I would have inspired in the ones I love.

As the weeks pass, I have no choice but to continue focusing on my education. I slowly become proud of myself as I start to smile rather than cry when I think about Stan, until one day, Mom comes to me and asks if I can take a break from studying.

"Donna just called," she says. "She was going through Stan's computer. You know, cleaning it so she could give it to someone else instead of throwing it out. I'm not sure who she's giving it to, but she found something he wrote for you. I don't know what it says, but she said she would send it, so check your email."

Shocked, I quickly check my inbox.

"I got it!" I yell to her, excitement rising in my chest.

His letter explains how brave I am and how inspirational I was to him because I never gave up after my accident. It mentions the butterfly effect and the book we all created for him. I feel warmth in his words. Unfortunately, the letter ends too quickly, with him admitting that his ability to affect the world was sure to end but that I'll continue living with the chance to make a difference. Here, he added a picture of a colourful, shimmering butterfly with an explanation that it reminded him of me, all bright and cheery. He clarified he was not pressuring me but hoped it might inspire me to create my own butterfly effect on the world or even continue his.

I blink a lot while I'm reading because there are many times I can't figure out if he misspelled a word or if my tears are just distorting the screen. After reading it a few times, I see it's about 50/50. He must have written this for me after the cancer had spread to his brain. The highest honour one can get is a message from someone claiming you as their inspiration during life's most challenging times. The tears on my face are primarily from the happiness that I was able to be there for him in his last days, days when I felt so blindly self-absorbed in my own life and progress.

There's so much that can influence someone. There are sprinkles here and there, from media to friends or family members, ideas, life experiences, hopes, and dreams. If Stan has given me anything, it's the belief that an impact doesn't need to be large to be meaningful. Simple acts of kindness can be more significant than they look. Instead, he gave many smiles and encouragement to continue moving forward. I want to be in a position where I can help people and do for them what Stan has done for me, but I have to focus on improving myself first. So, I put my computer aside and have a guiltless nap, resting with a calm heart that assures me I'm doing the right thing, even though it may seem lazy to some.

Walking through campus on a sunny day with Stan still on my mind, everything in my life floats away. Fewer trees are beside me than when I'm in the countryside, but they're still beautiful. Nature, placed anywhere, is beautiful and helps me relax. Walking to the Webster Centre to take a test, I hope it will involve more essay questions than multiple-choice. I feel pretty confident as I sit and review my notes. A wave of emotions are roiling inside me. I take a moment to sit back, take a deep breath, and look around at the new office. They moved the centre into the Student Union Building, and many more people are here. Sitting across from me is a young man around my age, studying in one of the comfy, dark blue chairs. I give him a quick hello to see how he responds and continue to ask if he knows much about this office.

"I'm here taking a test with the Webster Centre instead of in class like everyone else," I tell him. "But there are new people, like you, I've never seen here before. So, I'm wondering if this place doubles as something else."

"Oh yes! There are a lot of different offices here. This is the Student Union Building, so students can come here to study or have appointments with administrative support or counselling. A lot of the university's club offices are here too. I work right there," he tells me, pointing to the door on his left. "I study here because I like the atmosphere. It's quiet, and with it so close to my office, I can skip in there if I need anything like food or another pen. Come on. I'll show you." I follow him to his office.

He takes a key out of his bag and unlocks the door. It's a simple office with a tiny desk, chair, laptop, and a pile of folders. I glance at the door for a name, but it's blank.

"So then, what do you do here exactly?"

"Oh! I'm sorry. This is the Student Diversity Office." He pauses as if that explains everything, but I look at him, puzzled. He's a tall, white man; what can he possibly know about diversity? I tilt my head. *Maybe he's gay?*

"What do you mean exactly? What kind of diversity do you work with, and how does this office benefit the school? I'm sorry, I don't mean to offend."

"No!" he replies. "I'm glad you asked. You're not offending! These are good questions. All kinds of diversity! I know that I'm obviously a white man," he says with a laugh and a gesture. "I don't know if you can tell, but I'm also homosexual. We support the LGBTQIA+ community, and we try to support a lot of international students; it can sometimes be difficult to move to a different country where you're a visible minority." I don't bother asking him if it includes students with disabilities. I already know the answer is most likely yes. It wouldn't be obvious to him, though, that he should mention it, since my disability isn't quite as *visible*. The word stands out to me, reminding me how much my life would be different if it was visible that I had been partially paralyzed.

He continues, "So, this office is here for students to come to for help or guidance. We're trying to create awareness across campus, and across Charlottetown in general! Diversity here has been growing so much lately." He smiles at me, and I smile back. He is good at his job as a welcoming person.

"I love that! I didn't even know this office existed."

"Yeah, visibility is something we're working on. I think it's still a relatively new office on campus. But, hey! We're trying to get some students to volunteer and help spread the word. Are you interested?"

"I don't know… I put a lot of my focus on my studies, and to be honest, I'm straight and white, so I'm not sure how much help I'd be or even if I *should* help."

"Nonsense, we welcome everybody. Allies too! I'll leave you here so you can continue studying for your test. I have to study too, but here is my card. You can email me for more information when you get the time. No rush! And I promise not to demand too much from you. Whatever time you can offer, we'll take it. It could be for random events or when we need people to operate a table."

I thank him graciously and head back to my seat. This is precisely the kind of thing I'm interested in. Volunteering will help me move in the right direction to help people. I'll have to see if I can make any time to become a volunteer. Maybe I'll even learn more about diversity.

When I finish my test, Mom picks me up and takes me to my aunt's place to spend the rest of the day with the dogs. Before I nap, I take them outside and stand on the back deck. The sky is a soft baby-blue mixed with a touch of magic. Light, puffy clouds slowly drift. It seems almost as if they're going somewhere for a party. Maybe they're on their way across the Atlantic Ocean. A fatter, white cloud passes overhead, breaking my gaze and making me notice the tops of the calmly swaying trees. They're already at the party, dancing to the music of the wind. I laugh to myself. *Maybe the party is here.* Looking down at the two giant furballs running around playing, I know I'm right. The party is here, and I feel like a pretty wallflower. I take a deep breath and the Island air fills my lungs. I'm okay with being a wallflower for today.

My bedtime routine is getting repetitive. I stretch every muscle I possibly can before finally resting—legs, back, legs again, and neck. On to my arms; my left shoulder always hurts when I stretch it too much. It is still frozen and can't reach like my right, so I decide to leave it alone, not to hurt it. I feel the pain in my body, not just from my shoulders but from every muscle I've been strengthening since my paralysis. Usually, I become tired enough to close my eyes if I do these stretches and other small things before bed. For example, I might do fifteen sit-ups, focusing on core strength to prevent falling and injuring myself. No more than fifteen, though—not because my abs aren't strong but because my back isn't.

Once I finish my exercises and stretches, I sit on the edge of my bed and pick up my bottle of over-the-counter painkillers. I pour two pills out into my hand and blink at them. My pain is chronic. It'll always be there whether I like it or not. I can minimize it with therapy, but it'll never take it away. This means I have one of two options: live in constant pain and discomfort, or get sucked into a vicious cycle of drug relief. I think about this for a moment, wondering if entering a cycle of drug addiction should be a possibility for me. I mean, what is my life anyway? It's not like I can work full time. I'll always feel like a burden to society.

"All I want to do is sleep!" I scream aloud in my empty room as I continue to overthink. I decrease the pills in my hand from two to one to see if my body will become less dependent. I lie down and fall asleep just fine.

My bladder wakes me in the middle of the night. It's still weakened from the catheter from years before. When I'm back in bed, my mind stays awake. Eventually I look at the time and see I've been lying like this for almost two hours. I have physio tomorrow, and I don't want to look tired for her. *Why the fuck can't I get back to sleep!?* I stare at the dark ceiling. Closing my eyes, I assess my mind and body. My lower back has a little fire inside, my neck is stinging, and my foot feels like it's slowly dislocating from my ankle. I feel a tiny pulse in my arms and a slight shake over my skin as if I have too much energy. My brain is just tired; it's my muscles that are the problem. Without thinking about it, I get up out of bed and take the second pill I deprived myself of only hours before. I don't know why I have to overthink everything. Chronic fatigue is real, and it takes precedence. I still like the idea of reducing my need for painkillers, but tonight is not the night. *I need sleep.*

Sitting in class the next day, I take three small bottles of chocolate milk out of my bag to drink and help wake myself up. Sugar mixed in with some protein is my new coffee substitute since I discovered I react badly to caffeine. Using sugar to wake me up isn't a great habit either, especially because I have hypoglycaemia, but I don't care. Leave me alone. After drinking it so much in my first year, coffee makes me sick. *I have chronic fatigue; what else am I supposed to do?* These days, everything can kill you. I'm not drinking alcohol or caffeine; I don't lead a normal lifestyle. So let me have a little more sugar than I'm supposed to. At least to get through this morning—or until I graduate.

The professor walks in and starts his lecture. This class has an intense study regimen. Every week we have to read a book or two on human culture and reflections of anthropological fieldwork. This includes books on animal intelligence and a few others on human–animal interactions. After doing the readings we come to class, take a quiz, and discuss how they relate to our main topic. Reading this much makes me very tired, so it's a challenging class, but I'm learning how to handle it. I'm learning to read an entire book faster and not fall asleep as much in the middle of a page. Instead, I take more controlled breaks in between chapters.

In describing to us a past study on the differences between the intelligence of a human compared to that of a domestic animal, the professor uses the r-word, applying it in the same way as the formally known medical term for someone with a severe mental disability. Being raised in a household where the r-word was strictly forbidden, not only because it's insulting to others, but because it grossly misinterprets any level of intelligence, it makes me uncomfortable enough to speak up and ask that he stop. I don't like the word. Society has, over time, made it into a synonym for *stupid*, and it's used predominantly as an insult. As someone born in 1992, that's the only way I'll hear it, as an insult to others based on their perceived levels of intelligence. As I walk out of class, I take a deep breath, feeling my lungs fill. I have just done my own unthinkable: I spoke up in class. I didn't just speak up in a class, I openly questioned what my professor was saying. Overall though, I'm happy I said something. I calmed my thoughts. I was respectful, I voiced my concerns, and he easily returned to his lecture, rephrasing in a way I feel made his point more understandable.

As I step out I'm confronted by a fellow student who is waiting for me at the door. She thanks me for speaking up, saying that her brother has severe autism, and she and her family have been dealing with people like this for years. What the professor said is just an example of how many people still use this word without realizing the harm it does to others. Our society should know better now, that's no longer an accepted term.

"Unfortunately," she says, "people always think it's okay to throw the r-word around and judge a person's intelligence without knowing them first. So, thank you, it was nice to have someone stand up for others in this way."

"No, thank you for coming to thank me," I say. "I was worried I might have been disrupting the class by speaking up. I'm glad to know I didn't."

"Oh, no. If anything, you helped me focus more. Because of you I wasn't focusing on the fact that nobody was saying anything about it."

"I wish I could've said more." I laughed nervously. "But it took all I had to speak up that little bit. I'm usually quieter than this. He just hit a nerve."

"Oh, I know. Anyway, I have to head off. I just wanted to thank you!"

She leaves, and I stand there in awe for just a moment because I feel as if I've been influenced by her. By taking the time out of her day to thank me, she's given me more confidence than I've had in a while. Confidence to believe that I have it in me to speak my mind, even in a public manner. *I may not be the only one with these thoughts, and I wonder if I speak out more, maybe I'll find new ways to connect with others.*

* * *

After my first semester, Donna, Stan's wife, comes to visit. She heard from Mom that I want a tattoo of the butterfly in her husband's letter to me, and she offers to take me and pay for it in honour of him.

Christmas comes and goes, and suddenly I'm entering my next

semester. With more time to think about things over the break, I start to have more panic attacks again. Just a couple, but still more regular than before. *Or are they anxiety attacks?* I don't know if I ever learned the difference. I move to the internet to see if I can find out, and surprisingly, I don't find as much as I had hoped. The two terms are interchangeable, making any signifying differences hard to find. 'Panic attack' is the more proper medical term for it, sure, but that's not what I'm looking for here. I want to know *why* I'm going into the episodes, what's happening to me. I hope that if I can find the cause, then I can help calm myself on my own.

I can only find that one significant difference is the root cause of the attack, so I sit and focus on myself. I search deep inside to see what might be causing this tightness in my chest, starting with a body scan that lights up red everywhere. Many of my muscles are still in pain and discomfort. My brain, too, is tired, maybe more so than the rest. *Is the brain a muscle?* I didn't even make it to my feelings and thoughts. I feel a tightness in my chest that is indirect, with no origin or cause, but it's an anxious feeling that feels unsettled. I feel restless. Maybe my mind hasn't yet learned how to cope with my new, necessarily slower lifestyle. I feel like I should be busy, up and doing something, but my body is saying no. I need to reconnect my body and brain so they're closer to being on the same page. I stare at the wall and speak softly so no one can hear me outside my room.

"I know you want to be up and moving right now, but I'm sorry, I just can't. I don't have the energy. But that doesn't mean you're wrong. I understand why you think we should be up and doing things and making things happen, and it's okay to think that. From what I can tell, that's normal. But you have to understand that it's okay if we just sit here." I shake my head quickly, sitting, talking to myself. "You were smart enough to lessen your to-do list so that we can handle what we're limited to in a day. You can be smart enough to realize that there's no more that we really need to do. You don't need to feel anxious because there's nothing to be anxious about. Calm down." I take a deep breath, my eyes closed, my brows knit. This isn't helping, so I try one last thing.

"Okay, it's obvious you need to be in an anxious panic right now, so I will let you do that. We'll try it. Feel the anxiousness. I'm not going to stop you. Just try not to be anxious for too long, okay? Because we at least have *some* work to do, and if we don't have time for it, *then* you'll have something to be anxious about."

I smirk and take a second deep breath, letting the attack happen while staying grounded, staring at the wall. I let my brain feel what it is so determined to feel. I go along for the ride, feeling the pressure in my chest reach a high, a low, then heighten again until it slowly dissipates. In time, it leaves, and my brain rests in a recliner in the back of my head—only a few minutes, and I am back to my studies again, more slowly this time. I can't believe that worked. I don't know if it'll ever work again.

My second semester goes smoothly. I follow up my first religious studies course with another one that seems to be its direct opposite. It's called Hate and Evil. I laughed when I first heard it, wondering if we'd cover divorce in this class too. Instead, ironically, it covers many of the same themes as the first class. It also feels as if this class encompasses even more modern examples than the supposedly happier one did. Could the world just be going to shit? Maybe we're becoming more hateful and disagreeable the longer we live on this Earth. Of course, I may feel this way because I'm tired or have a recency bias.

Preparing for the end of the semester, I instinctively register for another, more advanced forensic anthropology and archaeology fieldwork course for the start of the summer. After counting up my course credits online, I decide this would be the last summer course I need.

My friends from high school will finish after next year, but I still have a couple of years to go. At this point, my benchmark is myself, so it isn't as important when I graduate. While I'm still friends with them, I don't see them nearly as much as I used to. Instead, I've been making friends here at the university. People who frequent the same study lounge as me since studying is my only hobby. I met a group of new people last year, and they've kept me around so far. I often see my friend Becca in this study lounge, where we talk and joke.

Speak of the devil. I'm studying in the lounge when Becca walks in. Seeing me sitting in a big chair blanketed with books, she heads for the chair beside me.

"You look like you could use a study break," she says, putting her coat and books down. "I'm just here for a few minutes before my class starts. How's it going?"

"Oh… it goes," I say. I roll my tired eyes, lifting my books slightly to show how heavy they are.

"Hey, I was talking to Nicole yesterday, and we wanted to invite you to come to a girls' night she's having this weekend."

"Really? That's so sweet. Maybe, if I can figure out a way to not be too tired, I can stay up late with you guys."

"Oh, of course, no, let me know. You're invited, though. I just wanted to let you know." I really want to be there and will have to figure it out. She adds, "We're making it a Disney night. Nicole still has a VCR, so we're bringing Disney movies we watched as kids. Maybe even sing along a bit. It should be fun!"

"Perfect; I have lots of old Disney movies. I'll try to pick one out that you might not have already."

"Totally up to you. Also, don't be worried about being too tired. If you want, you can stay the night and fall asleep during one of the movies. That's what we'll all be doing anyway."

"I won't be drinking either," I add, but I'm sure she already knows. I've told her before that I don't drink. I quickly change the subject before I make it awkward. "Do you guys really talk about me? That's so cute you thought of me. I'm going to love this."

"We talk about you all the time. Sometimes it's good stuff, sometimes it's bad." She casually shrugs her shoulders, and I laugh.

"Good, because trust me, it's not all good," I say, thankful that she feels she knows me enough to know that I have a sassy and salty side.

"Don't worry, I know," she says.

"Okay! Well, geez, you don't gotta be mean about it," I say, feigning hurt.

"Oh no, I'm sorry. I'm just joking. I thought you knew that."

"Of course, I knew. I was just adding to it. Please don't actually think you offended me. I hope I didn't offend you by making you think you offended me."

"You didn't offend me… or did you? You'll never know now. Maybe I was just playing it further, and I got you in the end."

"Good point. We'll never know, I guess."

"We'll go to our graves now, not knowing who got who."

I am definitely the one who got her. I squint my eyes at her. *Or am I?*

I return to my books after we say goodbye. She knows all about my brain injury and fatigue issues, she knows I don't drink, and she's totally accepting! There isn't much else to talk about in a room made for studying. Thankfully, Becca and her friends have welcomed me into their friend group as if I've always belonged. There is no judgement towards me for not wanting to party late into the night. They have no questions about why I'm not drinking. They don't pry into my daily schedule or wonder why I live as I do. They just accept me, for me. And I like them for who they are: unapologetically welcoming. People aren't all built or raised the same, as I grew up naively believing they were.

I grew up in such a tiny town, on a small island, in a big country, in a vast world. There's more to life than what I grew up around, and I find it very exciting.

* * *

Before summer ends, we have another meeting with the lawyers. This time, I'm allowed to sit in a separate room. I'm unsure if it's because they know it tires me out and they're being considerate or if they still feel my wrath from last time. I choose to believe it's the latter. While we wait, I make Mom explain to me, yet again, the difference between a mediation and a discovery, as well as everything else legal. I know I must know this, but I forget. I ask her if I've asked her these questions before, and she tells me I do almost every time. Even if my lawyers explained the proceedings right before, I always ask her to repeat everything. This must be her sixth time explaining the whole thing to me. The tests I went through, the lawyers, the part-time work for what we think will be the rest of my life, everything. My mind feels like it's overflowing with information: what I'm studying, how to manage my time, and how the brain injury might have changed, well, everything. Plus, all this legal information… it's so much to remember. I thank my mom for letting me remove an item from my brain's list of things it needs to keep track of.

I may never know what future to expect, but I don't think I'll ever work full time. I'm at a high risk of living in poverty. I can envision myself on the street, my body weakened even further by the cold, unable to balance my sugars with regular food, and sore from sleeping on a cement floor. Any of these things alone would be highly detrimental to me. It's a horrifying future, and I'm one fight away. I stand my ground because I know what I deserve, and I know the downfall I'd suffer if I didn't. Sitting in the little white room with my mom, I am left wondering why I feel like these lawyers seem to think so little of me and why I can't remember anything. Mom's so patient that she repeats herself so many times. A saint!

"Why can't I just be normal and remember?" I ask this out loud, tired of hearing my thoughts, and she answers me.

"I don't know, Kamya."

Chapter Ten: Social Justice

One day near the beginning of my fourth year, I wake up in a daze, go downstairs, walk on the treadmill, stretch, and make it to the shower, tired once again only an hour after waking up. Not just mentally and physically tired but exhausted by life. I sit on the shower floor with water rushing over me and let it wash away my tears. No one else is home, so I can sob as loud as I want. I cry because there's no reason not to, and because it's not hurting anyone. If no one sees me, my pride is safe, and my brave persona remains intact. Everyone thinks I am so sweet and brave, and the pressure I feel to keep up that identity weighs me down until it feels like I'm drowning. Maybe, by letting my tears of frustration out now, on my lonesome, I'll be less likely to lash out at someone who doesn't deserve it. Unfortunately, the people that do deserve my wrath don't exist.

Am I mad at the lawyers for needing me to go through tests as if I'm a rat? No, these tests are the only way for them to prove the effects of my brain injury and give me a proper settlement. It's not them putting me through the tests anyway; I'm doing that. The way I see it, they are doing their job, and their job is to make sure I'm not trying to get more money than I need or deserve. It's my job to prove that to them. *I can't be mad at them for that.* I shake my head in frustration. Am I angry at the driver who hit us? No, because they call it an accident for a reason. Who am I angry at? Myself? *I'm doing my fucking best, so leave me alone! I'm angry! Why can't I just be angry? Why does it have to be directed somewhere specific? Can't I just want a blinding, vengeful rage at how shitty life can be?* That's it! Life. I am mad at life.

I'm mad at the world, at existence. I know there's beauty in it, too, blah blah blah, fuck that. It's also shitty, unfair, and absolute crap; that should be acknowledged, too. And so I cry my eyes out, my tears spinning down the drain with the steaming water. I let myself see the darkness because it feels like no one else allows me to see it, and it's every bit as important as seeing the light. I'm tired of being strong. Stepping out of the shower, I realize something. I can consider myself like sugar. A little bit of sugar is soft, sweet, and versatile; I too, can be kind to people and flexible to help and connect with others. But I shouldn't worry about being too sweet and dissolving. A large quantity of sugar can be sweet, but it can also be as hard as a rock and difficult to break. Burned down, it's solid. You knock on it, and it echoes back.

Volunteering with the Student Diversity Office has, at least, added some sweetness to my life. It allows me to do something not just for me, and I love it. I crave this so much. I'm so tired of thinking about myself all the time. I decide to expand on this feeling and volunteer with UPEI's International Buddy Program. Students get paired up—international students with local students—to learn more about the university and PEI. As part of the process, we start with a single lecture about how to get the most out of the buddy experience. They tell us, Island students, the dos and don'ts from their perspectives, and to respect the fact that not every student might think like we do. Lastly, they encourage local students to make the most of it and learn about other countries just as much as we help others learn about ours. This last part, I think, is my favourite.

"Hello, everybody!" The coordinator greets everyone at the door before our meet-and-greet session starts. "Let me just explain a few things before you begin. You've each been given a short course on what to expect. We understand that not all people are suited for each other, so that's what this meet and greet is for. We want you to go around the room and talk to people. Don't just stay with the friends you came here with. Talk to someone new: if you realize they're not who you're looking for, move on to the next person, or you can visit me or another volunteer over there, and we'll find someone you can talk to."

I start walking around slowly, looking as if I have a direction to go, eyes darting here and there. I can see the discomfort in some people's eyes, realizing they just let someone they don't know put them in an awkward setting. I try to wave to a few people, briefly thinking that I, too, must be crazy to put myself in this room, while considering how this could be good for me since it might take me out of my comfort zone. Suddenly, I nearly bump into a girl who looks to be around my age.

"Oops! Sorry," I say. "I think I'm looking around me too much, desperately trying to find someone." I laugh.

"Oh my God! Me too!" She laughs back with a toothy grin. Her straight black hair is so smooth and controlled that she's not bothering to play with it like I'm playing with my messy blond curls. "Do you mind if I stay with you for a bit to look like I'm talking to someone?" she asks.

"Oh! That would be great! Who knows, maybe we'll turn out to be friends." I feel so comfortable that I nudge her, and immediately feel sorry that I'm possibly invading her personal space. Meeting new people, you have to think about these things, and I'm realizing I didn't. I blame the Island. We all grew up so close and personable around here.

We do it with good intentions, but some people might not like that; even some Islanders don't.

"Maybe!" she says, her smile unwavering. Not only does she not mind that I broke the physical barrier, but she also seems almost grateful. I try not to look so relieved.

"Well, jeez, let's start then! I'm an Islander, born and bred. I grew up near a small town about thirty minutes from here, in… that direction!" I point to an empty wall, imagining where I'd drive home. "It's called North Rustico. It's mostly a fishing village, but I don't live right in the village. I live a few minutes away, but I have a nice view of the water."

"That sounds so nice, I'd love to see that," she says. "I'm from Japan. I'm not sure if you know the city where I'm from. It's called Tokyo?"

"Of course, I know of Tokyo. That's like a huge city, isn't it?" She nods.

We continue our conversation and click immediately. She tells me her name is Chiyo, and soon we promise to be buddies in the program. She's only here for the school year, and became an international student because she dreams of seeing the world and meeting new people. I told her that's something I would love too, but I feel a little more stuck here, quickly sharing with her that I had recently experienced a brain injury, but hopefully not in a way that puts too much attention on me.

She shares her inexperience with meeting new people and making new friends. She likes taking herself outside her comfort zone and learning how to adjust. I smile and tell her I do the same thing. It's the best way to live life. Since she came here alone, she doesn't really know where to start, so I give her some ideas. If all else fails, I assure her that I'll be here for her, and she can experience what it's like to be a part of a PEI family. Immediately, we start to plan when she might meet my family. The next holiday is Thanksgiving, but I offer for her to visit my house this weekend to meet my mom first. That way, she won't feel so lost in a family gathering.

When Chiyo comes home with me after classes on Friday, she meets Mom and we all have a nice dinner together. The conversation is smooth. We learn that Chiyo is open to eating all different types of food, just like us, and she shares with us some of her own family traditions. Mom gets very excited when I tell her I already invited Chiyo to every holiday celebration while she's here.

"I have to warn you, Chiyo," I say, "my family likes to plan gatherings. Basically, if we're not at a family event, they're talking about the next one. You don't have to go to every gathering, well jeez, you don't even have to go to any of them, but you're invited to them all, so you can pick and choose if you want."

"Yes, we *do* do that." Mom laughs and adds, "This Thanksgiving is at my brother Trent's house. He has a big family, and has this large dining room table he built a couple of years ago to support large gatherings. He'll probably serve the traditional foods: turkey, gravy, mashed potatoes, sweet potato casserole, maybe some pecan pie. I think the guest list is at twenty-two, or maybe twenty-four, because I think Trent just added his daughter's boyfriend's cousin."

"Twenty-five if we add Chiyo," I add.

"Yes, it'll be around twenty-five then. A big one. I hope you're okay with that," she says to Chiyo.

"Oh my God!" Chiyo says. "That sounds incredible. Thank you so much. I can't believe this. How welcoming you are, inviting me to your home and Thanksgiving like this!"

I hope this isn't all too fast for her. It doesn't look like it, though. Otherwise, I'd happily ease up a bit.

After our long dinner, we go to bed. Mom already set up the guest room for Chiyo, and I apologize for not having the energy to stay up later. She tells me not to worry because she's exhausted enough from coming here and keeping up with the conversation at dinner. It baffles me as I remember that English isn't her first language. I breathe a sigh of relief and leave her be.

In the morning, I suggest we go for a walk before Mom takes Chiyo back to her dorm. I guide her to my favourite secret opening among the trees that leads to a field behind my house.

"This is the path I've been walking for the past year when the weather is nice. I try sticking to the sides to avoid stepping on the plants and ruining them. I'm trying to get used to a ground that isn't exactly flat so that I can challenge myself by walking on something other than a treadmill."

"Yes, you're so right! Walking outside is much better than being inside on a treadmill. More natural."

"If the weather's nice. When it's raining, my feet swell."

"It's so beautiful here." She gestures around her. The sky is a perfect shade of blue, and there's little wind.

"I love it," I say, "but most people my age who grow up on the Island leave the first chance they get. I don't know why. I usually assume it's for job opportunities, but I don't know. Everyone's different, I guess. Most return for visits, though, so it can't be that bad."

Chiyo and I continue walking down the second field. I tell her about my neighbour who works in these fields. He lives next door to us and works the farm across the street. I briefly explain what growing up next to a farm on PEI was like; I've always been close with my neighbours. Next, I ask her what it was like to grow up in Japan. She describes her parents' small apartment, with no guest rooms like in my home, but tells me it's an efficient space with everything they need and nothing more. With such a populated city like Tokyo, it's better not to take up space that people won't use a lot. I like that. People in North America take up way more space than we need to. We have some rooms we barely use.

She describes their school system and how much parents expect from their children. I tell her a good education has always been on my mom's priority list, but probably not the same way, especially after my brain injury. She shared some descriptions of Tokyo with me. When I turned my nose up at the thought of being among the tight crowds, she moved on to describe more peaceful spots I could visit outside the city that include more nature and history. We talk about our whole lives, being open with each other under the agreement that if one of us veers outside the other's comfort zone, she could speak up. Ultimately, we both want to share and know anything and everything. Finally, we make it to the end of the second field, where I interrupt her.

"I'm so sorry. I'm loving this conversation, but before we turn around to go back, I need to prepare you. I've only really walked this far a few times before, but when you turn around and see the view from this spot, it takes your breath away. I just don't want you to miss it, because the very first time you see it is when it's best. So, just a few more steps. Okay, turn!"

Turning around, we see we're standing at the end of a field that looks like it's growing wild for a season. The grass is long, bright, and luscious, with a sprinkling of wildflowers and lady's lace. Over the long-highlighted grass are miles and miles of empty air. Before us, our eyes reach infinite hills with fields of varying colours and miniature forests of evergreen, oak, and maple. A stretch of blue water is framed by a sky that sparkles just like the water but with a lighter shade. There are even a couple of white and light-green speckled dots here of friendly daisies. At first sight, it's a lot to take in, but in a huge, spectacular, and wondrous kind of way.

"See? This is why I love the Island so much." We continue taking in the beauty that surrounds us. "The people are great and all, but this, this is freaking beautiful."

"You're so right. I'll probably never see a place like this again," she says as she takes a few pictures with her phone.

"If you do, let me know! I'll have to visit it."

We walk back home, and Mom drives Chiyo home. I break open my books to make up for the lost evening of studying. I didn't even bother to tell Chiyo that I have another neuropsych exam coming up soon and that I'm worried about it. I kind of forgot, to be honest. I was having so much fun. However, now that she's gone and I'm in my room, it's all I can think about.

The following week, I'm back in class. Finding out that I have a test in my first-year English class on the same day as the neuropsych exam, I calm myself before I start to panic. These are extenuating circumstances, and I shouldn't feel guilty. This situation can qualify as a medical exemption since there's no way I can reschedule the day. If anything, I scheduled neuropsych exam before I knew the test date, so it gets precedence. Once the class ends, I approach my professor to tell her I can't make it to the test that day.

"Oh, okay then. That's no problem. It'll just be marked as incomplete," she says to me, so cavalier.

"No," I say to her, shaking my head. "I want to be able to make it to the test, but I have to go to an appointment in Halifax that I made a year ago. So I won't make it back in time to make it to the test, let alone study for it."

"Well, that's not my problem. I can't allow you to take the test on a different day. That's a breach of information and could lead to someone cheating."

"But I can't just not take the test. I'm not getting good enough grades in this class to be able to just get a zero on a test that's worth twenty percent!"

"Again, that's not my problem," she says. "Maybe you should have thought about that before skipping it. This has been on the syllabus since I gave it out in the first week. If you had come to me before I made the schedule and told me you needed the day off, I might've pushed it a day or two in either direction, but it's now on the schedule." I look down, thinking about how Mom only reminded me the other day that I have this exam booked. Otherwise, I wouldn't have known. I'm not at the level yet where I can organize my life so nicely.

Anxiety starts spreading through what I feel is my sad, damaged brain. *A brain so pathetic that in a first-year course required by every student, I'm not getting good enough grades to skip one fucking test.* I take a deep breath; my inner thoughts are mean, angry, and exaggerated. I just want to rip something apart, but I feel my lack of energy controlling me.

At this point I'm afraid I'll do more harm than good, so I pick up my things and glide out of that room, taking up as much space as possible while doing it. I know that I am being unreasonable to her. Still, I know she is being unreasonable, too, so I head straight to the Webster Centre. It's where I'd be taking the test anyway. I share what my professor said with the woman at the front desk. Hopefully, we can find a happy middle ground. In these offices, I feel like I can be a little more open about the appointment in Halifax and why I am so stressed about it.

"I'm so sorry about that," the lady at the desk says. "I can assure you that that won't be the case. Let me see if someone can help you now to put your mind at ease."

"Oh my God. Thank you. Thank you so much," I say as if she just saved my life. "I'll just sit here. I have time for the rest of the day to wait, until four-thirty when I'll get picked up." That gives me a three-hour window to meet with someone. I think maybe sitting will help me calm down before hopefully seeing someone.

The second my ass hits the chair I remember I planned to catch up on studying for my other class this afternoon. I can't do it tomorrow because that time is for another study. If I don't get to do both of those things, I won't be able to start studying for the test that I am fighting about now, and don't forget the afternoon naps I need to take. I take a deep breath. *Thank God my thoughts are just in my head.* They're so scrambled. I take a breath and tell myself, *It's okay. We'll figure this out.* It's not long before someone takes me to their office. At least there are good people to help balance the bad days. Balance. It's good.

* * *

Before I leave for my neuropsych exam in Halifax, we make an agreement that I'll write an extra paper to make up for the marks I'll miss from not taking the test. My head hurts thinking about how close I was to failing, quitting university, and living at home for the rest of my life. I'm being dramatic, I know, but it's a thought process I can't help going through. When I arrive I'm relieved to find that I've worked with this psychologist before, meaning I don't have to get used to a new office. I hold my breath for the test to be over, still trying my best and hoping it'll be my last. My head starts pounding within what seems like the first hour, and my arms begin to feel weak after three or so. I don't get a clock to look at, and even if I did, there's no way for my head to measure time in this state, but I know to expect this since it's my fourth time doing it. We spend a whole day testing my intelligence levels and measuring my fatigue only to ignore it. Finishing the day in that overworked and overtired state, I stumble from the little private office to Mom's car. I can't focus on anything other than lifting my legs and being careful about my ankles. As much as studying tires me out, I haven't needed to focus this hard on moving my legs since I was in the hospital. It seems like years before I reach the car door and fall inside.

"How was it? How are you feeling?" Mom asks as I struggle to find the seatbelt.

I manage only a grunt in response, having little strength left to speak. I feel excessive fatigue. This isn't even a lazy, hungover morning; I feel like my body is shutting down. My vocal cords are tired, and my world feels dizzy. I close my eyes to gain a little energy for Mom's questions.

"You know, you don't have to do this test in one day," she says. "I remind you of this every time you do it. It's a test that can spread out over three days. They just do it this way because you ask for it."

"I know." I struggle with my words so much that I know it's hard to make out. "But it's so fucking unrealistic take longer. I have school and studies, and I can't pay for four nights in a hotel, and you'd have to take off extra work, and I need to practise walking every day, and…" My voice fades, reminding me I was once mute, and I close my eyes as I get even more tired while listing my infinite problems again. I can't even figure out where I am on the list. My thoughts are angry, but nothing else matches. My speech is weak. I need to take things slow. Always taking things slow. Except for today, apparently. I feel like I'm supposed to do the impossible in these tests and do what I don't usually do in everyday life because they're too harmful. If I spread it out over three days, that would be three consecutive days of this! I would be even more exhausted. Remember, my lack of energy from one day bleeds into the next.

"Well, let's hope you're right, and this is your last one. It probably will be if this one comes up with similar results as the last one."

I turn my head toward her. "Really? You didn't tell me that before," I mumble. I wonder how she still understands me.

"I know. I didn't want to affect how you might perform. I wanted you to be able to do your best."

"I wouldn't have done anything different," I say. "I don't think I could have done worse. I'm so useless and dumb."

"Don't say that! If you're going to be mean like that then I won't give you the present I bought for you today."

"You got me something? What did you get?" My head is still resting on the seat because I can't lift it, but I try to open my eyes. "If you bought something for me," I say slowly, blinking as if my eyes weigh as much as a two-tonne truck, "what else would you do with it but give it to me?"

"I don't know. I guess I could return it, but you're right."

She hands me a small jewellery case, and I open it to find a new Claddagh ring inside.

"It's to replace the one you lost after your accident," she says.

"Oh! Thank you," I say, my eyes half-open, unsure how excited I sound. "I don't even remember what happened to my old one. That was the one I bought in Ireland when we went the first time. I loved it so much, too. I doubt it would fit me anymore anyway."

"You're right. They had to remove it after your accident and by the time you were ready to wear it again, I couldn't fit it onto your finger," Mom says. "But you have this one now! Well, try it on. I just made a wild guess, but hopefully it fits. It's white gold too. I think your old one was silver, so this one's better."

I put it on, and it fits perfectly. This ring represents my Irish heritage and reminds me of Grampie. It makes me happy, and it's hard to feel so tired and unfortunate when I'm spoiled like this by the best mother in the world. I smile and sit back, content. Still tired, but less grumpy. Calmly, I look out the window and think about my day. I wonder if I did any better this time, or maybe I did worse. What if my health is declining with how awful it is? Suddenly, my whole body screams at me in pain, and behind those screams come images. I'm lying in a bed, motionless, not knowing what's to come, that I can't walk or eat. I can only sit there, blind to the work ahead of me. If I had known what it'd be like, would I have even started to fight? I'm sure I would have—or wished I would have. The ability to walk and be independent is now, for me, a proud accomplishment, but the road to get here wasn't easy. Maybe it would've been better to stay in that coma.

The flashes continue: learning to walk, frustration in moving my left hand, missing home, crying in the elevator, and feeling alone. I do my best to take a deep, shaky breath without Mom noticing. The music is still low from when we were speaking just now. I gently shake my head to smarten up and quickly realize it's a bad idea because I'm too tired to keep myself from feeling dizzy. If my body feels more pain when I start dwelling on these memories, I should stop thinking about them. Turning to Mom, I ask her how long until we get to the hotel. I'd love to cry myself to sleep again while my saint of a mother sits in silence next to me, respecting my need for no additional stimulation.

* * *

I'm sitting in an exam room at the Webster Centre during finals. The room is so quiet that my mind wanders. My mind doesn't always do this, but maybe I've been too stressed this semester. I don't know. I sit back in frustration, thinking about a missing word to complete a sentence. I look all around the room because sometimes, if I stop thinking, it comes to me. This room is larger than others I've been used to, and it's completely empty. I'm very aware right now of how deserted it is. You could fit twenty people comfortably in here, and now, there is just little me in it. I am taking my exam and writing essays, forgetting painfully simple words. This is my last exam of the semester, and it's still hard to imagine I deserve any of this.

Soon, I'll be on Christmas break and in the second semester of my fourth year. If I hadn't been in the accident and had a brain injury, I'd be graduating in a semester. *That's so soon!* I realize many of my high school classmates ended up in places they also didn't expect. *I guess I'm not that different from the norm.*

"But I am," I say aloud with a faint echo of loneliness.

After Christmas break, my next semester starts gently. I decide to finish my required first-level credits this year with a first-level sociology course. Since I'm taking anthropology/sociology split classes up to the third level, it should be a little easier on me. I can't believe it's taken me four years to complete my required first-year credits—the same amount of time it would take a fellow student to complete and graduate from the program. With the second- and third-year courses taken, though, it evens it out a bit. I shrug at the thought. *I think I've learned enough over these last few years to know that I can't compare people. Everyone's different and unique, and what works for some doesn't work for all.*

But do I really understand how different everyone is from each other? Or am I just getting full of myself, pretending I've found the secret answer to everything?

Walking out of the Student Union Building one day, I'm faced with a poster advertising Black History Month with a time and date for an event at the campus bar. I quickly decide to attend this bar's open mic night, celebrating Black History Month.

After my night at the bar, I can't help thinking about individuality. I went into the open mic expecting to hear a specific type of dialogue. I came out having heard stories of Islanders, like me, constantly searching for people who understand what it's like to be judged solely on their looks and familial background. I've strained to find people who understand me too, but for far different reasons. Every person's history, upbringing, and mental state make them unique. Without even looking at differing ethnicities, we are still all our own human selves, all uniquely different, built and shaped into who we are today.

Growing up, I was taught not to discriminate because we're all the same, but now, as an adult, I know that can also be detrimental and fragmentary. Suppose I expected everyone to have the same privileges as me. In that case, I wouldn't be actively seeking change and removing barriers to make the world one I want to live in. I would also be missing out on learning other ways of living. If this isn't the world I want, I need to help change it. Lyrics from "Raise a Little Hell" ring in my head. The song I used to inspire me to walk now empowers me to fight against harmful societal systems.

My brain injury is a factor that's slowly defining who I am, whether I like it or not. Although I'm glad not everyone has to go through what I've been through, finding someone who understands has been challenging. Instead, I've been connecting with people in general, looking at their potential. We all have brains that make us walk, talk, eat, sleep, communicate, study, and many other things, but no two brains are the same. Scientists can't study the human brain efficiently because it's too impossibly divergent from human to human.

Generalizations in human society can have their benefits, they can help us begin to understand new people having no information before. But it's become evident that general conclusions made too broadly can also hinder many. It has led to many different groups' misunderstandings, prejudices, and discrimination. It's our habit to make assumptions that we know as facts or actual knowledge because it allows us to base our opinions on data when in truth, we have none. We do it most often when we don't even realize it. Maybe we're letting these generalizations guide us too much when, instead, we could allow the unknown to open our minds to new learning.

Easter comes, and we all enjoy our last holiday with Chiyo before she goes home after exams. We've had a fun year. She gets along so well with my family and me. Over Christmas, we had the amusement of my family attempting to make Japanese food. It might not have been as classic, but it was still delicious. Eating non-traditional food for our Christmas Eve was fun. Reminiscing, we talk about our favourite foods over Christmas. We all vote that the noodle-iced cupcakes were the best.

Grammie turns to Chiyo and says, "Well, you can come back any time, Chiyo, and we'll make more cupcakes for you. We can even do the whole thing again! With the food and all. That was so much fun!"

Chiyo laughs. "Well, maybe not *all* the food. Maybe I can bring back some food for you from Japan!" The whole room roars with laughter. It was painfully obvious that none of us had made Japanese food before, and Chiyo isn't afraid to make fun of us for it.

"You fit in with us so well, Chiyo. We're going to miss you!" Aunt Izzy says.

"You can come back any time to revisit the Island. Or maybe we'll come and visit you," I add.

"Yes!" She turns to the room. "I told Kamya that whenever she's in Japan, she can email me and tell me she's coming so I can give her a tour around Tokyo. Of course, the same goes for all of you, too. If anyone visits Tokyo, I'd love to see you again. We could just get some supper together or something. We could meet at a perfect noodle spot near my parents' place."

At the end of the party, everyone says goodbye to Chiyo while I stay back. I'll have a chance, I hope, to see her once more before exams start and we're both too busy. Chiyo and I sometimes walk around town since neither of us has a car, and we plan to do that again before she leaves. When we finally say our goodbyes, we exchange emails to keep in touch. She makes a last dinner for us of treats her mom sent from Japan.

Summer comes quickly, and soon I'm back outside enjoying the colours and fresh air. The extra physical space creates freedom in my brain and gives me a break from the pressures of studying and overthinking. Resuming my part-time work at The Toy Factory, I restock shelves silently before opening. I love the smell of the wood and toys around me here, but soon, I will have to grow up and search for jobs that might lead to a career. I wonder if one could even get a career with part-time hours. I should at least try, though, right? Next summer will be my last summer before I graduate. I should start branching out and figuring out what I might want as a career for the rest of my life.

The university keeps advertising apprenticeship programs and business start-ups, but it is all outside the range possibilities for me. There's no way I can work in an office while simultaneously being a student, so summers are all I have to work with. Even with that, finding a program that will allow me to work part time might be impossible. I need to think about what I want and how to get there. Do I want to work in the tourist industry for the rest of my life? If so, I could stay. Bill and Karen have taught me a lot already. But no, I don't want a career that has me on my feet for hours a day. Usually, my feet and back get even more sore by the time summer ends, and I wouldn't want this for longer than two months.

Of course, a desk job would create its own set of problems. My neck starts killing me when I study too much with no breaks. So basically, I'm always sore. Working at all, even part time, will be difficult. Maybe, then, I can pick something I enjoy. I can at least pretend to have options. Before I leave The Toy Factory at the end of the summer, I tell Bill and Karen that this will be my last summer. It hurts to tell them I'll be moving on, but when Bill tells me how proud he is of my decision to start seeking a career that will hold me for the rest of my life, my heart fills with joy and love. This place is indeed a home for me, and I will surely return for visits.

Chapter Eleven: Domestic Labour

Walking out from making preparations at the Webster Centre, I look around the big building to take it all in. I'm only two years away from graduating but will surprisingly miss this place. Soon, I'll be in the real world where I'll have to figure out what to do next in my life. Since the accident, I've been able to disguise myself as a student, living at home to save money. All my other problems have seemingly been in the background instead of realistically running the show. I wonder if I'll be able to continue that after I graduate. Will I ever get my settlement from the insurance company? Will I find a career? Have kids? Get married? What kind of life will I have? Does it matter if I fit in with the social standard?

I pick a table in the shade and sit down, looking to soak in the campus atmosphere while I rest my feet. Soon, a young man comes and asks if he can sit with me, explaining he has just come out of the office area I was just in. I share with him that it's where I take my exams, not wondering if he'll judge me—I'm past that. He surprises me when he tells me he just started university here and will soon be doing the same thing. I quickly explain how it works, reassuring him that he's off to a good start by visiting the offices within the first week of classes.

"What is it, if you don't mind me asking, that makes you need to take your tests there instead of in the classroom like everyone else?" he asks.

"Oh, when I was a teenager I had a severe brain injury, and now I have chronic fatigue. Of course, there's more to it than that, but I require extra time to take tests and exams in this case. I get time and a half. That's been a reasonable amount of time for me. I'd get too tired if it were any longer."

"Wow, I'm sorry to hear that." This is the typical response I get when I start sharing information about my brain injury with new people.

"It's okay. I'm dealing with it…" I wave my hand and try to reassure him. "You'll figure it out too, I hope. I suggest you go to them for help if you're struggling. You can make appointments for counsellors in the same place. It's kind of convenient."

"Thank you! I appreciate you sharing your wisdom!"

"Oh God, what else would I do with it?" I ask, slouching before continuing. "What about you? What makes you not able to take your tests like everyone else? You don't have to tell me if you don't want."

"No, that's okay. I have Schizophrenia. Since I was about eight."

"I'm sorry to hear that," I say. "I have no idea what that must be like."

"Well, I'd imagine you have a little bit of an idea. After all, it has to do with the brain, which you're pretty much an expert on."

"I don't know… all brains are different, so I doubt I know much. All I know is people see me and have no clue! I taught myself how to walk and talk well enough so that it's not super obvious I was partially paralyzed at one point in my life, but now I realize that's bad, too! Because everyone assumes I can do more than I feel capable of. I can only assume you have the same problem because I wouldn't have guessed anything from looking at you."

"Yes, you're right to assume that. And you're right; it can feel harmful to be treated like everyone else when you're not, but it's better than the alternative."

"Exactly." Looking down, I add, "Would it be awful to ask if you could tell me what it's like? To have schizophrenia?"

"Well, there are stereotypical things, like voices in your head, although that doesn't happen as much to me anymore. When I was younger, maybe. There's also the inability to focus well on particular tasks—that's what I deal with mostly now—and there's extra fatigue, too," he says, gesturing towards me and my mention of fatigue. "Of course, probably not to the extent you have it. It's just tiring because my mind works overtime thinking about so many things. It can be exhausting."

"I bet." I make a mental note for myself to learn more about schizophrenia, knowing good and well how difficult it'll be to find good information. "Do people ever look at you and think you're so brave? Like you're like some kind of saint for going through everything?"

"For sure. Or at least the ones I tell my problems to."

"Yeah, me too. But I never know what to say, because it's just like any other Tuesday. I don't really have a choice, do I?"

"I know what you mean. It's definitely an everyday struggle. There's more to it than just *getting better*."

"I never know what to say to someone when they ask if I'm *all better now*. Like, yes… but no… it's more complicated than that." Then, finally, I look back up, "Oh! I should probably warn you because when I take my tests, I do better when there are no other distractions in the room. I'd imagine you'd be even worse for that. Sometimes, I get study rooms where I'm alone, but other times, I get a room with others. Of course, it's one thing to be in a room of thirty other people taking a test, but when there's only three or four, it's so crazy easy to hyper-focus on their pencil moving, their legs shaking, or anything like that."

"Ugh I hate it when people shake their legs. I understand it usually helps them focus better, but it's annoying!"

"I know! Anyway, I think you can probably request to be alone. It might be a bit harder to figure it out, and you might not get it every time, but you should ask. If you don't, you might get stuck in rooms with four or more other people. Honestly, the longer I'm here, the worse it gets, and you're just starting; you should make a point of asking to be alone for a test or exam."

"Thank you, I'll do that," he says as he starts to get up. I pack up my stuff too; I have class soon and want to leave in plenty of time to find it.

"Thank you for stopping by," I say. "I'm happy to have met you. It's been a nice chat! I'm sorry, what's your name again? I'm awful with names."

"Dan. I'm happy I met you, too! I hope I can meet other people as open as you are. If so, I might just love it here!"

"Yes, I'm positive you will. Just surround yourself with good people." I nod to him jokingly, books in hand. "I'm Kamya." When he walks away, I write his name down so I don't forget it.

In class, I can feel blood rushing through tired bones. I distract myself by preparing my books. The name of the class is Critical Thinking of Psychological Research. I can think critically about that! I'd love to learn more about psychology, and it'll be nice to understand how some people dispute it. The public will often soak up any reasonings for what they don't fully understand. It gives them comfort. If only people could learn to find comfort in the unknown as well. That's one of the things that I think makes us uniquely human—the mystery. We must acknowledge something as an unknown before we have the curiosity and courage to learn more about it.

"Good morning," my new professor says as he walks up in full view of everyone. "To start our class, I want to play a little game. I want you to look at the person sitting next to you."

I am on an edge seat and look to the only person sitting beside me. She's a young woman with dark curly hair, and she's already looking at me. We nod and laugh together to confirm our partnership. Next, the professor goes to the board and writes a series of questions for us to ask each other. *Where are you from, what's your major, where would you like to visit,* etc. They are simple queries, and he encourages us to ask an extra question or two if we think of it. After I finish copying the questions, I turn to my partner. "Okay, I'm ready when you are!"

"I'm ready too," she says. "So, where are you from?"

"I'm from the Island. Born and raised, not much to it. I grew up about thirty minutes from Charlottetown. What about you? Where are you from? I detect an accent."

"I'm from Italy. English is my second language."

As I write down her answer, she turns to her notes to get to the next question. While I'm studying anthropology, she's studying psychology, and we're both scheduled to graduate next year. Then she asks me where in the world I'd like to visit.

"Italy!" I say. "Actually, my mom and I have always wanted to visit Italy." Then, laughing, I calm down to ask her the same question.

"Here," she answers. "I've always wanted to visit Canada. Not really PEI necessarily, but Canada for sure."

We barely get through the questions because we get caught up in learning about one another. She offers me a tour of Italy, which quickly develops into a graduation celebration. When the professor starts talking again, we trade papers to answer each other's last questions to finish faster. While we're writing, I quickly mention the Student Buddy Program and how I got a lot from it last year.

"I'll be your partner," I say, "or we can even skip the program and just be friends, and I can fill that role for you anyway since you're only here for one semester and don't have much time to waste."

By the time class finishes I have a new friend, Elena. All because of a silly class exercise that made a point about general assumptions and prime seating.

The classes I've chosen for this semester excite me. I may be a nerd to think this, but the first week of classes is always fun. I even brave another English class, A Survey of Literature to 1785. I think it could easily be considered a history class, which is how I like to think of it. We start by exploring some of the earliest English texts preserved throughout history—long epic poems to read and decipher.

Along with the psychology class I'm taking with Elena, my third class this semester is a special topics class in masculinity studies. With most of my required courses complete, I can now cover other subjects I'm interested in. I plan to make the most out of my time left here, taking fun electives and ensuring I get a broad education.

Masculinity studies is fascinating; it's under the Diversity and Social Justice department, something I've always been interested in. Maybe I can learn more about masculine problems and better understand and figure out what makes this group's situation particularly challenging. What problems do they have? Well, we spend weeks reading articles about the extremists. Men who believe their position in society has diminished to make room for others, blah blah blah... There are always extremists in every movement, I guess. In class, we focus on articles that teach us where the term "masculinity" most often comes up in modern society, and how the concept of masculinity can be also very harmful to them, as it is to women, but in what sort of different ways.

By the end of the semester, I'm collaborating with a group for a final presentation. We have to choose anything related to masculinity as our main topic. We plan to meet up with suggestions, so the day before I'm sitting at my computer trying to think of some. It's tough to research when you don't have a topic. I look at Lindor on my left, and to my right, Littlefoot. *These two are such great study partners!* They are so peaceful and quiet while I study. I do what I often do when my brain freezes like this—I call for Lindor to get up so I can pat his head. I pet Littlefoot more when I study because he's usually closer. Sometimes, though, I need the big guns. Being the great dog he is, Lindor gets up slowly and lets me pet his soft ears before going to the door and asking me to put him outside. It's almost as if making him get up reminds him he needs to pee. I groan because that wasn't my intention at all. When Littlefoot joins him, I decide I have no choice.

Putting the computer aside, I let them out quickly, trying not to let in any cold air. I stand there, trying to enjoy the fall view, while remembering that I miss doing yard work with Mom. As soon as I sit back down, an idea comes to me—women who work in masculine-dominated workplaces. It's something we didn't cover in class. I quickly look up some articles before retiring for the rest of the day.

The weekend before our last week of classes, when my group will present our project, we host Thanksgiving at our house. Mom decided to host this year so we can enjoy our one holiday with Elena, my new Italian friend I met in my psychology class. We celebrate, in honour of her, with Italian-inspired cuisine. We call it Italian-inspired because of the lesson we learned after making Japanese food for Chiyo. Elena makes carbonara. The spread includes various pizzas, meatballs, breads, and cheeses. It goes the same way most of my family gatherings do: lots of food and chatter. Homemade limoncello is out for everyone to try. Elena gets along with my family very well. We all toast her, thank her for coming, and share how sorry we are that she'll be leaving at the end of the semester and miss our family Christmas. By the end, we're all tired. Even Lindor, now thirteen, isn't afraid to show how tired he is from all the excitement. After the guests leave, we turn in early so he can get some extra rest. When we wake, it seems like Lindor barely slept. The next day, he's worse.

"He won't go outside," Mom tells me.

"What do you mean he won't go outside?" I ask. "He must have to pee. It's been all night! Did he pee on the floor?"

"No, of course not. It's been years since Lindor peed on the floor! He's a good boy. I guess he's getting older, though. I didn't notice anything when I got up."

I agree with her, but I look around the house to see if I can spot any pee hidden or dried up. I come up with nothing. I don't think the floors have ever been this clean. I approach Lindor and crouch down.

"Lindor, baby, do you need to pee? Your bladder must be bursting." He looks up at me with his brown eyes, head still resting on the floor. "Come on," I tell him. "Let's go, get up. I'll go outside with you." He struggles to get up, so I help him. He's had arthritis in his hind legs for a while now. It's common in old labs.

He follows me outside and starts to show some excitement but stops short at the top of the steps that lead to the grass. I yell for Mom.

"It's the stairs. He doesn't want to do the stairs. Maybe his hips hurt."

"He won't do three steps?" She says to me, drying her hands on a towel.

"No," I say, looking into his eyes. "No, he won't."

Mom takes a breath, puts the towel on the table, and comes outside. She lifts the eighty-pound dog with a strength I've hardly witnessed before and carries Lindor down the three steps. Then, as if it's nothing, she goes inside and shuts the door behind her. I sit on the chilly bottom step and watch Lindor search for a spot to pee. His bladder was full, alright. He pees for what seems like a solid five minutes.

"Okay, baby, let's go back inside. Come on, I'll help you up the steps if you want." Lindor comes to my legs, sniffs me, looks at the steps, and back at my legs.

I've known this dog his whole life. I trained him, and I'm the person who talks to him; he's my best friend. We share an unspoken language. I know his answer without him doing anything. So I pet him and tell him it's okay.

"Come on, then. Let's go to the downstairs door," I say. "There are no steps there. You can't stay out in the cold."

At first, I wonder if he'll even follow me down the hill, but I look back and realize he's already passed me. Just when I start to see his age, he turns back into a puppy. He often hangs out with me in my study/treadmill room, so I set him up there and go upstairs to tell Mom what happened and that he should probably spend the day downstairs. She agrees and tells me she'll call the vet to make an appointment.

"He's pretty old, Kamya," she says softly. "He could have just hurt his leg—but maybe we should consider that he might be at a point where we need to put him down."

"We'll see what it is, but I know. I don't want him to be living in pain."

I go downstairs to spend time with him. I will no longer be able to make my presentation tomorrow. After quickly sending my professor an email telling her of my situation, I sit on the floor and put his heavy head in my lap. He's always been here for me—my best buddy. I can't help the tears rushing down my face as I tell him repeatedly that he's a good boy and I love him. His body shakes from the pain he's in. I sing his favourite song, "Galway Bay" by Celtic Woman, and he slowly falls asleep in my lap. I camp out on the couch at bedtime so he's not alone and try to sleep with one hand on his fur until morning.

In the morning, we go to the vet. After Mom manages to get him in the car, it's clear he will not be jumping out. When we get there, the vet nurse offers to take a table to the car to get him. It doesn't take long for the vet to see us. They perform tests, expedite the results, and soon return with the news that he's likely bleeding internally and in a lot of pain. I don't hear much, just that something has ruptured and options presented to put him down. Since Mom and I have already discussed this possibility, she takes the lead.

I bury my face in Lindor's fur, thanking him repeatedly for how much he's been there for me. After my brain injury, he learned quickly not to pass me on the stairs and to stay quiet while I studied. His body has always been there to steady me when I felt like I might fall, and to lean on if I'm getting up off the floor. I dropped my cane earlier than expected when I got home because I knew he was there to steady me if needed. I thank him so much, yet not enough. Soon, the vet is standing by with a needle in Lindor's front leg attached to a syringe. She tells us we can stay, so Mom and I stand beside him, four hands petting his fur. As the vet empties the syringe, his eyes slowly close, and he lies in complete soft peace.

Returning home, we feel a sense of peace, knowing he's no longer in pain. I go to the room where I spent the night with him and cry. When I get a moment, I look back at my emails, forgetting all about the presentation I spent the last three weeks preparing for. I'm surprised by a reply email from my professor, who sends condolences for my loss. I'd been bracing for whatever kind of punishment but read instead that she has three dogs and understands how difficult this must be. A second email explains that my group agreed to present my part for me. Since we collaborated throughout, with our notes accessible for everyone to read, they have an easy enough time doing it and claim they don't mind. She wishes me well and hopes that I make it through finals to Christmas.

I wake the following day with a deep sadness. As I get started on the treadmill, an inspirational song comes on my playlist, one that I have added recently: "Fight Song" by Rachel Platten. Through my feelings of grief, I belt the chorus out at a pitch I barely knew I could reach. I've come so far, and there's still such a long way to go. I've done more than I give myself credit for.

I have to be strong and recognize my strength. I'm still in the process of taking my life back. I'm not completely independent yet. I probably won't be until after I graduate from university and move out of my mother's house, until I get a car and drive myself to my own appointments, until I can help others as they've helped me. I think of how my grandmother's been driving me to appointments and to work. She's more than earned any help she gets from her family after having five kids and thirteen grandkids. She basically created us, and we'd be nothing without her. I've earned nothing. I take a big, focused step on the treadmill in honour of taking my life back—one that doesn't drag and one that says I mean business. I belt out the next chorus with even more power and volume. *I'll get there.* I've come too far to stop now. There's a little fight left in me anyway—enough, I hope, to make it to where I can recuperate and gather more strength for the next battle life has to give.

After I shower, I sit on the couch to start studying, rotating my ankles first since they are in extra pain today. My right one does okay, but my left is not completing the full circular motion that it should. The ankle spins 210 degrees and makes a sharp, straight cut back to the start. *That's not what I told you to do, ankle.* It shouldn't be doing this. Trying again, I put all my effort into telling the ankle to do the full circle rotation. It shakes in protest. I stomp my foot, giving up. *It's been years! This fucking life. Fuck, fuck, fuck. I'll figure this out eventually, hopefully.* Practising the motion helps over time. Shaking it out, I tell myself to ignore this problem while I place my computer on my lap.

Sitting in my new Psychology of Women class with snow falling outside, I feel unprepared. Lately, my study method is to read the relevant chapter before the lecture and then make notes about what the professor covers. Then, I reread the chapters, highlighting those sections so I can quickly go over them before an exam. I don't know how it happened, but I couldn't read the chapter before class today. As a result, I have no idea what we're discussing.

So far in this class, we've covered the basics of female-specific problems in psychology. The last thing we did was delve deeper into how women differ from men. More information has been collected on men because, historically, women weren't allowed to participate in research. As a result, there haven't been enough scientists to recognize or care that women's mental and physical realities or concerns might differ. I had enough medical problems with my period cycle alone to know this is true. From what I can tell, everything we're learning in this class is painfully real and annoying. Maybe that's why I didn't read the chapter. Maybe I'm protecting myself from being upset about which subject might come next.

"Today, we're discussing domestic problems and disparities in the household," the professor starts. "I don't mean domestic abuse, which we will discuss later on. I'm talking about housework. Emotional labour, childcare, and how women are expected to excel in the workforce and still do most of the household work.

"Studies show," she goes on, "that women are often the ones to know when to pick the kids up from school, remember grocery lists, and do the shopping. Also, notice and clean things when they are dirty, plan and prepare meals, schedule and attend doctor's appointments, and all those essential things that help a household function."

I sit in silent awe. I knew it was bad, but I didn't think it was this bad, and I certainly didn't know there were actual studies and proof behind it. *Are you kidding me with this?* I look around. *What is being done about this? Women are expected to be self-sufficient, but most men don't even know how to do their own laundry or make their own doctor's appointments?* It can't be all men. Based on the men I know, I am sure they know how to care for themselves. But also, out of the men I know, it's true for those who are married at least. I spent most of my time growing up with a single mother. I never considered what living with a husband would be like.

Sitting at home later that evening, with the chapter in front of me and a highlighter in hand, I get back to these thoughts. *Is it true? If I expect to marry someday, will I have to be ready and willing to take on most of the housework and look after a grown man?* I can't help but think of how much housework I don't do now. Do I know how to do that, run a household? I've never thought about these things before. I've never thought of them as a problem. After my brain injury, I faced some big problems: number one, walk again; number two, study and figure out how to get a career. Now I find out I'm supposed to be learning how to be a housewife, too? *What the fuck.* I'm never going to marry if that's the case.

I've had so much work to do every day since my accident. I am constantly looking at the bigger picture. The future that everyone aspires to. Happy, triumphant in your own way, and satisfied with the amount of work you did to get there. I've come so far. I always think, if I just do this extra thing every day, it will get better! But there's always another thing to add to that list. Another stretch, another exercise, another thread of hope that things might be better. And at some point, it might. But at what point does that stop?

I've always thought the thing holding me back from connecting with a man would be my parents getting divorced when I was young. Not that their marriage ended badly, but I think it's made me sceptical, as I'm sure it does for many children of divorce. Or maybe because I can't stay out late during prime dating time to meet anybody. I've thought about the difficulties of motherhood with my fatigue levels, but never, *never* did I think I'd have a problem with a fucking adult relationship, just because society hasn't yet recognized the importance of teaching a man how to run a household. If having a husband will be this much work, am I losing my ability to get married, too?

The whole world isn't like this; men are competent. There must be men who know how to look after themselves without a woman. If I focus on my ability to look after myself without too much help from another, I should be able to find and fall in love with a man who can do the same. There's hope yet. I can't let this brain injury hold me back from anything else! It's ridiculous.

When my thoughts turn to my mother, I start to think of how much of the housework has been put on her since James moved out and I had my accident. She's allowed me to put all my energy into my healing and studies, doing all the extra duties herself. I put the book down and leave the room.

"Mom, I think I should start doing housework again," I say, thinking about how I'll need to learn to do my own housework because I don't like living in a mess. If I wouldn't expect someone to have me do it all, I shouldn't expect them to do it all.

"Really?" she says excitedly.

"Yeah. I was just thinking about how, eventually, I'll need to learn to take care of myself and do my own cooking and cleaning. I appreciate you doing it all for me, and I probably won't have the energy to split it 50/50 or anything like that because I'm still busy, but I should do little things here and there. You shouldn't have to do it all."

"Oh my God," Mom starts, "you have no idea how happy I am that you're saying this. Yes, there are definitely things you can do! You can do laundry and cook some meals. There are dishes in the sink right now if you want to do them."

"Woah," I laugh, "I can't do anything right now. I'm in the middle of studying. I just had this thought and wanted to come and share it with you before I forgot it. I'm in the middle of a page highlighting right now. But! If you leave them there, I can do them when I'm done!"

She agrees and I go back to finish my chapter as quickly as possible so that I can start my new task. When I return, I see that the dishes are already clean.

"It was bothering me, having them sit there," she says.

I laugh at her and turn to put a load of laundry in instead. At least I still remember how to do these things from before the accident. I just have to get my body used to them again.

After accomplishing another productive day by going to bed on time, I wonder how long it will last. *This isn't so bad.* But after a few days, I start to feel a little off. I've overdone it, and something is wrong, but I'm unsure what. I begin my nightly routine, reaching for my toes. I notice my swollen ankles and bend over to poke at them. I move on to my back, completing my usual stretches, still limited by my left shoulder. Once I finish and lie down, tears fill my eyes. My body aches immensely.

It feels like a truck has rolled over me; I've been productive lately, but now it's all hitting me. Everything hurts; it would be a relief right now to be swallowed by the depths of hell, cuddled by lava and comprehensible pain. What I'm feeling now isn't understandable to those who have never dealt with chronic pain. It feels like I imagine phantom pain to feel, except that I have all my limbs. I can't think of anything else to describe it. My legs are there, but not there. I am very aware they are attached to my body, screaming at me to recognize them and enticing me to smash them to prove their existence. Distracting myself with my belly, I compare it to my thin, underweight figure after the accident. I prefer being soft like I am now. It feels less fragile, but deep inside, I know it's not how I should want to look, and this is not how I should feel.

I take some pain medication, lie down again and stare at the ceiling, tears blurring my vision. Would anyone understand my nonsense? My cheeks are wet in no time, tears washing away the face cream I just put on. All I can think of is how grateful I am that no one can see me crying because I'm alone in my room. Alone. *Always alone.* Most people my age have a significant other and might even live with them—I wonder what that's like; I wonder if I'll ever have that. Would it be so wrong not to? My self esteem is so low, I can't help but tell myself I don't deserve it.

* * *

The trees on campus sparkle an Island green as branches dance in the wind. I'm walking toward the chapel. Of course there's a building on campus for students to pray—that makes sense—I just never needed to know about it before. Here is where I take yoga classes with a friend. I hear yoga is supposed to heal, and I have much to soothe. My legs are flexible since I already focus on them in rehab, but my arms and shoulders are more limiting. For example, when Alex, the instructor, tells us to reach for the sky, I raise my arms but can't hold them up. It hurts too much in that position. Healing and relaxing, indeed.

"Before you go, I want to introduce you to something new," Alex says. "I know I've guided you into some chakra meditations before, but I've yet to guide you into a real, deep, meditative state. So, I've invited someone here to campus to help us accomplish that. He'll be here later today, around three o'clock, to talk to us on video chat about Transcendental Meditation (TM) if you're interested. He'll answer any questions."

Leaving the class, I think, *why not?* I return for the video chat and afterward sign up to meet the meditation instructor in person. I have nothing to lose. Nothing else is working for me. My pain management is spotty at best, and I'm tired *all the time.* I've found that the more rest I get, the better the pain is, but I get tired so quickly. After years of rehabilitation, everything still tires me out. That yoga class was an hour long, and even though I took a little nap before and it was supposed to be relaxing, I had to close my eyes again after. Now feels like the right time to learn how to meditate correctly from a professional instructor.

Mom drives me to campus in time for the introductory meeting with Paul, the meditation instructor. There are nine of us sitting to hear his presentation. The presentation is impressive. Not only does he go through the cost and process, but he also presents us with recent scientific data based on Transcendental Meditation that suggests it can improve brain activity and sleep patterns. Based on the atmosphere in the room and the scientific data, I leave the class with the same thought on my mind: *why not*. There is no pressure to complete the course, so what's the harm in trying it? It costs some money, but it'll be worth it if it helps me even a little. I discuss the price with Mom on the drive home and tell her it's a weekend course, so she'd have to drive me. She agrees, saying it's my money and time, so it's my decision. I'm so grateful to have her on my side.

The training weekend goes smoothly, and I pick it up quickly; I wonder if my experiences make me more in tune with my body. After yoga the following Thursday, Alex comes up to me. Since we took the TM course together, he's wondering how I'm doing with my practice. I forget that we're supposed to check in on each other to ensure we continue doing the meditations twice a day. Paul warned us that some people have difficulty fitting it into their schedule, but I figure it's a small ask.

"I know you told me about your accident and your chronic fatigue," he says. "I think you also had some sore body issues that make yoga hard. Are you feeling any better? Are you still practising TM, doing your two meditations a day?"

"Yes, I'm still doing them," I say. "They're helping me, actually. Not drastically, but it's noticeable for sure. I'm pretty excited about it! I used to be tired ALL the time, and I hated it. Now I get at least a few minutes a day when I don't feel tired, and it feels amazing. Of course, I'm still sore, but that's another problem. My body's dealing with having to move after being dormant for so long and being paralyzed on top of that. I still hope it'll improve, but I don't know, it might be a lifelong thing."

"Where is it? Like, where is the pain?"

"Oh gosh, it's all over, but I guess the worst area is my knee right now. I twisted it or something. I don't know what I did, but it was a while ago and I've been going to physio and focusing on it there. It's been acting up these last couple of weeks." I gently touch my knee to show him.

He looks down at my knee. "You know, I've been learning this new Reiki technique. It's supposed to be good at relieving centralized pain. I'm wondering if you wouldn't mind me trying it on you? I can do it right now if you're interested. Of course, I have no certification, so that would be completely voluntary."

"What does it entail? Like, what do I have to do? I'm pretty tired from the class and haven't had the chance to do my afternoon meditation or nap yet."

"Don't worry," he says. "It doesn't require anything from you. You can just sit there and do nothing. All the work is on my part."

"Well, I don't see why not then." I walk with him to get some chairs and sit down. "That's actually been my guiding motto this year. It's how I decided to try yoga and why I decided to try TM. I've just been telling myself, *it can't get worse, so why not at least try everything and anything I can to feel better?* I think it's been working. I like it anyway; my body seems to agree with natural methods."

"That's cool! I'm delighted to hear you say that!" he says. "Okay, make sure you're comfortable, and I'm going to place my hand on your knee, with your permission, of course, and then I'll expel my energy through the palm of my hand into your knee. Our bodies are full of energy. Sometimes, we need extra energy to heal. If I focus my energy on coming through my palm and into your knee, you can use it to help heal the area. There's more to it than that, but that's the short of it."

I take a moment to make sure I'm fully comfortable with this man, then I take a seat next to him and roll up my pants to expose my knee.

He asks me to place my whole leg on his and sit back. I feel like he's offering me a free spa treatment. *What does it matter if you don't have high hopes? Maybe you just don't understand the science of it yet. Maybe the science of it hasn't been covered. It doesn't mean it won't work.* As pain courses through my body, I tilt my head back and think of how badly I'd love for the pain to be gone, if even for a moment.

"How's that feeling?" he asks.

"Not bad. Your hand is warm. I like it." For now, the rest of my body is in more pain than my knee, so I have nothing to complain about.

"Tell me about your accident. Was it a car crash? Did you say it was a car crash? If you don't mind me asking, I don't want to bring up any bad memories."

"It was a car crash," I say. "And it's okay, I don't mind talking about it. I don't know if I have any PTSD from it or not. If I do, it's from the process of getting better, learning to walk again, dealing with insurance companies, and going through these neuropsych tests. But the accident itself? I don't remember a thing."

"Really? You don't remember when the car was about to hit you or being on the road?"

"Nope, not a thing. I might remember small details from the morning of, and I know why we were in town, but nothing other than what people have told me." My hands start flailing around as I talk, like any Islander does when having random conversations with people, but I try not to move my knee. "Mom wrote a diary for me, too, while I was in my coma, but I still refuse to read it. She could burn it for all I care. I'm okay with hearing some stories, but the image of me lying in a coma is one I don't need."

"Wow…" He says quietly. I start to panic. I've shared too much, and I know it.

"Oh my God, I'm sorry. You just learned a lot about me really fast."

"It's fine," he reassures me. "It comes with the job, teaching this yoga class and dealing with people. I work at the Student Diversity Office too, as you know. I love talking to people and letting them spill their words all over me. I encourage it."

God, he would make a good life coach.

I can't say I've never had suicidal thoughts. I'm sure that most people have thought about it at least once in their life. I wonder if I would ever go to such lengths. At the end of a couple of neuropsych exams I remember that I was given a private questionnaire about suicidal thoughts. Since it was always at the end of a long and hard day, with the topic of suicide in front of me, those thoughts were strong enough to make me cry even though I hadn't thought about them on my own before—besides perhaps once or twice in the middle of the day studying or right before bed, when I was tired and feeling extra useless. With those times in mind, I can't say I never thought of it. I curse my stubborn attitude though, because in these moments I usually conclude that I have no choice and just can't. I always feel the need to get better and prove the world wrong more strongly than I feel the need to give up. *The world is what's wrong, not me.* Sometimes, though, I wonder if that's better, and those thoughts scare me just as much. If I don't feel like I have the option to kill myself—is that good or bad? Am I losing an opportunity to escape, in more ways than one?

This is why I'm learning it's important to find other escapes, ones that I can see are within my realm of possibility. Yoga might not be my favourite, but it's brought me to other places that are becoming methods of safe escape. TM is different for everyone, I'm sure, but to me it's not only a brief daily escape. It's healing and restful, just what I need. I used to nap every couple of hours, and now I meditate for twenty minutes twice a day and maybe giving myself an hour to nap afterward if I need it. These are hours I am getting back. I'm so glad I'm brave enough to search for different things that might help. I should remember this moving forward, with my focus still on graduating from university and figuring out my future.

* * *

I feel my eyes blur the pages of my textbook while sitting in the student lounge. The weather has been getting nicer, so I'm wearing shorts, and the book sticks to my skin. It's time for my second meditation of the day, so I peel the book off my bare legs. When I put the book on the ground beside me, I look back to my legs to see that it left an imprint, as if it were still there waiting for me to read. *Ha, that would make a good tattoo.* I've been thinking about getting a tattoo to celebrate my graduation, something to look forward to and show that I've made it so far: finally realizing my dream of graduating from university and not letting a brain injury or learning disability stop me. I've had so many books on this lap over the years. I'm surprised there's no permanent mark from them, but a tattoo can be that permanent mark, reminding me of how much work I did.

I am taking a class called Abnormal Psychology this semester. As I review my notes for the final exam, I reflect on the myriad ways a human brain can behave. What is abnormal anyway? To me, it is just an illusion. I don't believe in using the word *normal*, so of course, the word *abnormal* also seems like a falsehood drilled into us by society. I understand how it can be helpful in some contexts but I can't see why this concept of *normal vs not normal* is used so literally. It rules us in society, leads us to make assumptions rather than allowing us to see the full truth, and can make some people feel so lost and alone. Mental conditions that doctors know less about are labelled *abnormal*. To what end? To pretend it has a name and they know what they're talking about? Under the concept of *normal* can't we also say that it's *normal to be abnormal*? Normal for all of us to be different, have different brains, different bodies, and require different forms of help?

After putting my books down to head to the bathroom, I turn around at the door to pick one back up to take with me. I don't want to miss any precious studying time sitting on the toilet. After a few minutes, my phone rings. I know it's inappropriate to answer a call on this seat, but I'm alone in this two-stall bathroom, and it's just Mom—I'm sure she won't mind.

"Hello?"

"Kamya, you got it! Your lawyer just called, and they met today with a judge, and you got it! You got your settlement!!" She shrieks at me on the phone.

"What? *What?*" I'm suddenly even more glad I'm alone in this bathroom. It's been six years since the accident. "Was it what we hoped for?"

"I don't know the exact amount yet. Your lawyer just called with the news. He's calling back in about thirty minutes with more details, and we have to go in on Thursday to sign a few final documents. So you can ask him any questions then if you want. Write them down if you don't think you'll remember."

"Woah." I feel a bit dizzy. Years of my life, and I've always felt there was no end in sight. "So wait, you mean no more tests, no more studies into my brain and how awful my body is? I don't have to continue being repeatedly reminded how dumb I am and how useless my brain injury has made me. I can focus on positive things now?"

"You're not useless!" she says. "But, yes! No more tests, no more appointments in Halifax, no more physical tests on your body, no more neuropsych exams unless you want them. It sounds like it's all been worth it, and it's finished now!" A tear slips down my cheek, fast-tracking to the chin. "Where are you?" she asks. "I think we should celebrate! Go out to eat or something. I know you're studying for your finals, but can you do that?"

"I'm in the bathroom, actually." We both start laughing. I leave out the fact that I brought my book in here with me.

"Well, get off the toilet! Wash those damn hands and pack up your things! I'll be there in an hour!"

I'm still laughing as I wash my hands and take a moment to stand in front of the mirror, thinking about the situation I was in when receiving such an important phone call. I feel light headed. I had my second meditation recently, so I shouldn't be too tired. There is just so much to think about. After I steady myself on the counter, I leave to pack my stuff and meet Mom by the bus stop.

Once I finish my finals and the papers are all signed, one of the first things I do when I get my settlement is buy my first car. I'm almost twenty-three and going to university thirty minutes from my home. I haven't even been able to get a crappy used car yet. I hold my head high, knowing that I can now drive myself to my own therapy appointments, get myself to work, and if I want to go out to meet with friends or go on a date, *I can drive myself.*

Summer comes again, and I'm grateful that I still live at home. Unable to find any programs that support my part-time-only limitations, I decide to take the summer off instead. My student loans can cover my tuition. I'll worry about that after I graduate. I use this time instead to rest and finally relieve stress. I sign up to volunteer at a local seniors' home one or two days a week to improve my resume and help me keep busy. Still, I'm glad to have extra time to see Grammie and continue our lunches, as she'll always be my number-one old person.

When I show up for my first shift, the volunteer coordinator meets me at the entrance. "Hello! Are you Kamya? I was the one emailing you! Let me give you a little tour!"

I follow the coordinator on a tour of the large building. We visit many rooms, including the chapel, the dementia wing, and the common areas. We end up back in the lobby.

"We're pretty well staffed at the moment," she says, "so you have your choice of places to go. You can accompany some seniors on a walk outside. You can ask people if you can join them in their rooms. You can go anywhere or do anything!"

"I think I'm most interested in the dementia wing," I say. "I don't know if they get many visitors, but I think I can handle it well."

She brings me back to the dementia wing, reviewing the door's entry code and other basic rules.

"This section is closed off with a secure door at each entrance to prevent anyone from accidentally disappearing," she says. "From what I know, they're just like everyone else. Their families visit when they can. They eat their meals in the dining area and mostly return to their room to watch TV or rest. You'll have to ask a resident care worker (RCW) to see if you can take someone for a walk. They will have a better idea of what each person is like."

Walking into the wing, I find a few RCWs cleaning the tables and counters in the dining hall. They tell me they've just finished breakfast and introduce me to a few slow eaters still sitting at their tables. After saying hi, I sit down to relax my feet, which are already hurting. I wonder what I was thinking taking this on, when an older woman comes to sit next to me and start a conversation.

For the rest of the summer, this lady is the one that I spend the most time with. We walk, sit in the sunroom, and talk about our families. I swear that besides a few comments about never knowing when her family visits or what day it is, she's just like any other lady I might meet. I calm her down when she panics about not remembering simple things and remind her where she is from time to time. We become fast friends, and others always see us laughing together. When I'm ready to leave and start classes again, I hug her goodbye and hope she'll remember me in some way.

Chapter Twelve: Graduation

"Mom, can you come help me make my bed?" I ask and sigh with my forehead against the wall, but I turn right away for her to follow me because I know she'll come. I can fucking drive by myself, but it's still a struggle to make a bed sometimes.

"Thank you so much for helping me," I tell her as she pulls a corner of the sheet too far to her side. "I'm so sorry. I know I usually make the bed by myself. Usually, I can make it by taking breaks and lying down on it between layers." I laugh awkwardly because it's true. That's how I do it. "Just, today I have a lot of things to do, and I don't know why, but I'm so tired." I try to reason with her.

"You don't need to explain anything," she says. "I don't mind helping you out now and then. It makes me feel useful."

After we finish, she returns to what she was doing, and I sit on the bed, organizing the books around me. Thoughts of my slow progress and imminently changing future flood my mind, unwelcome. I can't even make my freaking bed on a semi-busy day. There is no question this body can't work full time, at full speed, or full potential. Remembering I graduate this year, a sense of uselessness and sorrow follows.

I stretch, cracking my back without trying. I rub my neck, constantly sore from looking down and studying, and glare at my pain-riddled ankles. I feel like I need to rip them off my body. I've been neglecting it and prioritizing school; no wonder everything fucking hurts. After I graduate, I can put more time and focus on my body again. It's nice to have a plan, however small. I can't even begin to imagine how different my postgraduate plan is from those of others around me. So, when people discuss which schools they'll attend next or what kind of postgraduate programs they signed up for, I congratulate them but stay quiet. When they ask, I say I don't know yet, but I do. I just don't want to share.

Walking up the stairs for lunch, I can see Mom has a spark of determination in her eyes, just like I do when I'm about to show her a documentary I know she'll probably hate.

"I was thinking, Kamya, about how you asked me to help you make your bed the other day but then felt guilty about asking for the help. You shouldn't feel guilty! I have a hard time making my bed too," she says to me randomly.

I laugh. "Did you just finish making your bed and have trouble doing it?"

She gives me a guilty look, biting her thumb and says, "No, but my sheets are waiting for me."

I roll my eyes. "Come on. Helping someone make a bed isn't so bad. I can do it if you promise me lunch." I know she's going to make me lunch anyway.

"Deal." We head to her room.

"Really, though," she continues while separating the sheets, "you have to think back on how much you've accomplished since your accident. Remember when you were at QEH, and your physical therapist asked that theoretical question about what you would do if you signed up for the Make-A-Wish Foundation?"

"Yeah, that was crazy, it wasn't like I was dying."

"No, she didn't mean it that way. Organizations like Make-A-Wish aren't always for kids who are dying. Some are for kids who are just living their lives in hospital and going through hard times, which, at the time, you were."

"I guess, since I was under eighteen, I could have applied for something. I spent my seventeenth birthday in a hospital bed, and you still made me do therapy that day. I still don't think I would have wanted it. Even now, I think that'd be exhausting."

"Well, you're technically an adult now, walking. You're even driving yourself to your appointments," she says. "But what did you tell her you'd ask for?"

"I don't remember... I think I wanted to have a tea party with my favourite celebrities because I'd probably never meet them in person otherwise. But I don't know. I also think being in a room with a random group of celebrities would be funny. Who was there? I think an actor, a comedian, a musician, and there were two others, but I can't remember them now."

She laughs. "It sounds like the start of a joke."

"An actor, a comedian, and a musician walk into a tea party and..." I laugh too. "It'd be interesting to see how that would end up. I don't think I'm important enough to be invited to that. I would've wasted a wish. Others deserved it much more than I did. I'm fine!"

"Exactly, you're doing great. That's my point. You've come so far. You just amaze me. I think about that conversation sometimes and about your answer. That's still such a simple wish after all you went through."

I smile at her. I have no other response. I hate it when she does that. She's putting me on a pedestal for surviving. *I had no choice.* If I had a choice, do you think I would have put myself through daily pain and anguish? Through trauma and flashbacks? *Hmmm, maybe I do have PTSD.* No, I don't think I would have, even if it made me a saint.

People fight every day, and I don't mean only those in situations of war or the like. I'm talking about the everyday person, them included—people who live their daily lives experiencing depression, dealing with anxiety, and battling societal norms; people who leave in the morning feeling sad but take on the world anyway. *Those people.* They fight daily and don't get put on a pedestal. Every human is fighting their own battle, varying in difficulty from one day to another. When they fight, they fight in silence. It can be a regular part of humanity. I am not the only one who deserves credit for this. I don't want it if no one else gets it. Life is hard, and everyone should understand that.

Returning to my bedroom, I continue to think about all the world's problems. With all the new thinking and focus on social justice, many issues are slowly being addressed, but not without difficulties. Young generations always get a backlash when trying to advocate for new ideas. But things *can* change. They *can* improve. If a new generation sees the benefit of exposing a problem, let them express themselves. Parents can influence all they want; they can raise their children and share how to understand the world. They can even encourage better education and resourcefulness when it matters. It's where it reaches a point when they're telling youth they can't change the world; that's when they're being hypocrites. You can't give us years of better education only to tell us we don't know things or give us the confidence to speak only to silence us. *That's the whole freaking point.*

I guess I can see where parents and older generations have a point too, but is their reluctance to change because they're tired of the fight? With each new generation, there's the possibility to move forward. Still, it takes large numbers to make it anywhere. And I get it when older generations advise us not to talk about our problems too much. My mind goes back to my brain injury and my life after. Discrimination is out there, whether we like it or not, and people judge. Not only that, but your future can depend on those people, and you don't want them to think less of you. Dan, the student I met in the student building that one day, was right when he said, "It's better than the alternative." I'd love to live in a utopian society where everyone can be their authentic selves, scars and all. Still, we don't live in that world. We live in a world where preconceived notions are embedded in our minds, whether we consciously choose them or not.

But there's hope. There's always hope. Letting people in can be magical. When it's just one or two individuals, society's ideals don't matter as much. Usually, when I open up to someone, we connect in weird, unconventional ways, and that's so beautiful. Change builds slowly and quietly in the shadows of society. Once you talk to enough strangers one-on-one, young and old, out of the public eye, you realize you're not alone. I love that most people in my life can have these types of conversations; it's one of the reasons I love them so dearly. We can speak to each other in a way that respects and celebrates our individuality.

My heart swells when I think about seeing my friends soon. We're meeting to discuss plans for a graduation trip together. I am one of the last to graduate, so we've put it off until this spring.

"On our road trip to Montreal, we should pick one activity we each want to do there, so that we can all be sure that we have fun and get the most out of it," says Becca at her house later.

"Oh, well, then mine is definitely skydiving," says Sarah.

Samantha is next. "I don't know what mine will be… I know we all want to go to the hobbit houses so that one can be mine."

"No, you can't do that," I interrupt. "We're there for a week, and we already agreed we all want to do that, so that can be the one thing we all pick together."

"That's a good point, Kamya. I like that," says Becca "Tattoos can be my thing because I'm the one who came up with the idea."

"I forgot about the hobbit houses! And the tattoos! Ahhhh! This is going to be so much fun," screams Sarah, and we all laugh.

"Jennie isn't here, and I think she said she wants to come too, so I'll just have to catch her up on this after," says Becca.

"So, what are we doing for tattoos?" I ask excitedly. "I'm already planning a graduation tattoo but can get two in the spring. This one can represent friendship for me, maybe."

"What tattoo are you getting for graduation?" asks Samantha.

"I'm getting a book on my lap to represent all the books that have been there while studying." I laugh.

"I like that," says Samantha. "I don't know. Why don't we take the lead from Becca's idea of each thinking of something so that nobody's ideas get left out?"

"Or, like, a theme, and we all get something within that theme?" Sarah suggests.

Everyone agrees on this idea, and we discuss it further. Since getting a tattoo is a big decision, we decide we should pick something sooner rather than later. I leave the meeting exhausted but with time to nap before getting together again tonight to drink and socialize.

Later in the evening, the room quiets as we start a drinking game. Even though I get no excitement from being forced to drink from my glass filled with pop, I love our drinking games. To me, they are important bonding time with my friends. I never have to worry about people going overboard because I know they can take care of themselves. They always plan for designated drivers, and usually, I'm not the only sober one in the crowd. We are each given cards we're supposed to imitate so the others can guess the word on the card. Mine says *hummingbird*. I quickly think, *that's easy*, and start flapping my arms as fast as I can move them. Nobody guesses a thing, so I flap harder.

"Come on, guys, this is so easy!" I say to the group. Both arms move as fast as they can go.

My arms start getting tired, so I pause briefly and try it again while humming.

"Hummingbird!" someone shouts.

"Yes! Holy crap. I can't move my arms anymore! How did you not get that right away?"

"Well, because I had no idea what you were doing. One arm was flapping like a maniac, and the other barely moved. It was just, like, sitting in the air."

My heart sinks, and my throat swells instantly. They're talking about my right arm; it was moving like crazy, and my left arm was only moving a little. I completely forgot the left side of my body had been paralyzed. The connection between the left side of my body and my brain doesn't work as it should. Embarrassed, I tell the next person to go so I can suppress my tears in private. *This will never go away.* As my throat starts to hurt, I walk to the kitchen to refill my glass and compose myself. By the time I reach the kitchen, I am glad I left because my eyes are overflowing with quiet tears.

I can't blame anyone but myself. I forgot! I should've thought of a different way to represent a hummingbird. I should've just hummed! Right from the beginning! Someone would have gotten it. No matter how much I improve and work on things, it'll always be there, and I can never escape it. A part of my brain is gone. I'm thankful it's not apparent; people can assume it's simple human error most days. I'm sure everyone's already forgotten about the incident, but I'll always know, and I'll always see it. I hold onto the counter and take a deep breath.

The tears dry before they're able to fall. *This is ridiculous; it's not my fault.* It's a weird, unusual situation, and I must move on. I turn to notice that someone has followed me into the kitchen.

"Are you alright?"

I straighten up and smile as if nothing had happened. I hope my friends aren't worried about me. "Oh yeah, of course! I'm just refilling my glass." I walk back out to take my seat again before I have to answer any more questions.

The rest of the party goes swimmingly. They easily forget about my disabled hummingbird. Before we leave each other, we discuss our neighbours in the US. With an election approaching, American politics is in Canadian news so much now. It's all *Trump this, Trump that, Hillary this and that too.* I don't even know either of them. Who cares? Does my opinion really matter? It isn't my country.

"We *should* care, and we *should* be aware. It might influence us somehow!" Someone pipes up.

Everyone agrees. I guess this election is more significant than I thought.

My family doesn't often talk about politics since I think we try to respect different views. Still, sometimes, my friends will talk about it just enough to ensure we all stay aware and informed. There's so much false information shared in opinion pieces and social media. It's good to have people around you who remind you to research for yourself. It encourages me, at least. When I get home, I pull out my laptop and see what I can find on the topic. It might not be my country, but this can be practice in learning more about politics in general.

First, I search the country's political structure, which, as it turns out, is similar to ours in Canada but still more complicated with all the different states. Then, I search for their haves and needs as a country. Finally, I make it to the candidates that people could vote for. After a tiny amount of research, I gain enough perspective to converse with people. Still, in the end, I can't stop thinking about the strong opinions of both parties. With only two significant parties in the United States, and just a handful of politicians who aren't Republican or Democrat, it's impossible to have a minority government there—or even a minority opposition. I could search for hours, and I'd still only find extreme opposing views on the two main candidates, Trump and Clinton.

Here in the political realm, I find a good snapshot of one of the ways modern democracy is failing us. People don't always have the time or energy to put in hours of research to inform their vote. It's so hard to find accurate, unbiased facts about these candidates because everything is about publicity. You're supposed to choose using candidates' promises and assurances, but how can you find those if opinions and media cloud them? No one can know what a leader will do for a country until it happens. Sure, the leaders don't always follow through on their promises, but that doesn't mean we just ignore them. Is voting for someone better than having a leader chosen for us? Of course. But we're not seeing the whole picture if we don't admit that our modern democratic system has flaws. The little research I did was more complex than it should've been.

I think of my father, who lives in the US, and others I know there too. It might not influence me personally, but this election might impact people I care about. On the other hand, the US is on the verge of having its first female president. And if they elect a woman as their political leader, I am sure Canada isn't far behind with another woman prime minister! That would theoretically double our options for electoral candidates. I close my eyes and hope that whoever they elect does what is best for their country. I know it's about more than just gender.

* * *

After Christmas, I find myself in the bliss of a romantic relationship. Adam and I can't stay away from each other. I attend classes, study on campus, and stay at his house frequently. This is my routine for weeks, until one night when I get up to use the bathroom at his house, turn on the lights and find a fuzzy black area blocking at least half my vision with the lights on. *This again.* My eyes have bothered me at times while studying, and when I am tired, but never during the night in the middle of a rest cycle. Have I been depriving myself of that much rest by dating this guy? I usually go to bed before him. I can't understand how dating can tire me more than being single. It's the little things, I guess.

Maybe I'm just not getting as many naps or as much rest. That's the only thing I can think of. I like Adam, though. I don't want it to end just because I'm not getting enough rest. By the time morning arrives, I've decided to talk to him about the issue, and he agrees that maybe we should adjust some things so that I can spend more time at home and get the rest I need. Arriving home, I finally decide to make an appointment with an eye doctor to confirm I'm not slowly going blind. It's such a confusing problem.

After taking some eye exams, the optometrist tells me it sounds so strange since my eyes seem normal, and that it might be a mirage or my brain might be playing tricks on me. It may be associated with how tired I am. If it happens again when I'm not feeling tired or if it doesn't go away after rest, I can feel free to come back and do the tests again, but for now, it isn't a problem she can fix for me. *So it's a mirage then.* That's what I suspected, as a joke, but it really is! I didn't even know brains were capable of such things. A mirage would make sense if I were lost in a desert without food or water for weeks, but I'm just living my life. I'm tired from studying, but isn't every other student doing the same? Am I really *that* tired?

Maybe now would be a good time to visit a psychologist and possibly address my problems. Mirages sure don't sound like a good thing. The last time I visited a psychologist, she agreed that my life was hectic and adding to it could be more detrimental than helpful. I agreed at the time, but I will graduate soon, and once I do, I'll no longer be overwhelmed by studying. Maybe I should revisit the idea. I take a moment to picture myself stepping into the psychologist's office, and that's it. My chest tightens, my mind races, and I feel frozen and nauseous. A heightened vibration gently echoes under my skin. My eyes painfully squeeze shut. I can't. There's *no way* I am stepping foot in one of those offices again. Where I'll be tested? Made to be tired? And worked over until I feel like I can barely stand? And I want to do this again, voluntarily? *No.*

I realize now that I was right. I must have some sort of PTSD. Maybe it's something I can work on in the future, but I guess to be tested and treated for PTSD, I'll have to see a psychologist. *Good luck.* Seeing a psychologist would probably be excellent, assuming it would solve all my problems. Still, it doesn't work like that. My progress is always slow. I guess I'll have to start alone. I mean, what kind of help would I get anyway? Would they give me pills to help me in the odd time when I panic or have an anxiety attack? Oh, hell no, I don't want to be put on any medication—by a doctor who can barely prescribe meds to a normal person effectively, let alone someone who has had a brain injury and experiences drugs in unknown ways. There's a reason I don't drink or do recreational drugs. It isn't just because the doctors advised me against it, but also because it makes me feel weird. I lose too many senses and too much of what little control I have left.

I close my eyes to stop myself because I know what I'm doing—I'm talking myself out of it, making excuses to not seek help. Psychologists can help; I know it. I've seen proof of it in other places. Maybe I can't motivate myself to do it now, but perhaps someday. At least I can take myself out of an attack. I don't want to take medication to ease my symptoms of PTSD. All I'd like is someone to talk to, maybe. If something comes up again after I graduate and I have more time or energy, I can address it then. I don't have time to add any more appointments anyway. I'm still attending at least four therapy appointments a month. That eye appointment was an extra one that has already set me back.

I take a deep breath. My panic eases slowly but my body is still frozen. My face is wet with tears, and I realize I've been crying. It's not over yet, the panic. That thought of walking into a psychologist's office brings back way too many unpleasant memories. It triggers something—the pain, the sense of uselessness, the strain for hope. It all comes back. I sit in silence, trying to find my way out. More rises to the surface instead. More and more problems resurface until I distract myself with plans after graduation.

What kind of career ambitions should I have after I graduate? It doesn't make sense for me to do any further schooling. Comparing regular pay for someone who works part time with the price of education, I immediately realize it's not worth it. Okay, so I shouldn't do any further schooling unless it's something I decide I want. The muscles in my face loosen into a frown. I don't want to be a student forever. Being a student for over ten years makes sense if you come out of it with a doctorate or a profession, but it's taking me six years just to finish undergrad.

The following day, I walk out of a test filled with long essay questions and stop to see if Alex is in his office. Something to occupy my mind might be what I need.

"Hey!" I say when I see him. "I'm just stopping in to see what's happening. Are there any special events coming up that I should know about? I need something to take my mind off things."

"Hello, stranger! Yes, actually. Mental Health Week is in May, and we're having an event at the bar to celebrate. I'm trying to gather speakers to share their stories and share some positivity about things they've overcome. I was going to email you about whether or not you'd be interested."

"Speak? In front of strangers at a bar?" The thought of it is bewildering, but it would certainly take my mind off anything else.

"I know, it's a big ask. That might be why we're having difficulty getting people to sign up for it. But please think about it. Email me what you decide. I'll keep looking anyway!"

Later that evening, while washing the dishes after supper, I think, *Why not?* That's been my philosophy before and look where it got me! I don't know what kind of person I'd be if that hadn't been a guiding principle. *What if I end up needing to be a public speaker?* I think to myself. In that case, won't a safe space during Mental Health Week be the perfect place to practise? I have to do it. Now I just have to figure out if I have a story to tell. I find some time from studying to write out a small speech just to see where it ends up and if it has the potential to become anything. After emailing Alex to say I'd be happy to do it, he tells me to keep it to five or ten minutes maximum. I wouldn't want to be up there longer than that! I'll aim for the former, maybe, to be safe, with extra time to take breaks, pauses, and freedom to speak slowly. Hopefully, that will prevent me from fumbling too much. I spend a reasonable amount of time working on it, and of course, I turn to Mom for help.

"I don't know how to do this. It's such a big story to tell! How can I cut it into a short, sweet speech? This is my life, and years of work. I don't know how to shorten it and not include all the tiny but important details."

"It's easy, Kamya! Just shorten it. Do the *Reader's Digest* version. Start with one paragraph at the beginning and move on from there. I know you can do it. You have so much wisdom to share with people, and now you finally have the chance to do it."

"That must be a saying from your generation, 'The *Reader's Digest* version.' I don't know what that means. Every story I've read in *Reader's Digest* in Grampie's basement growing up has been a long-ass story! That makes no sense! I need your help. Will you edit it with me?"

"Of course I will," she says, laughing because she knows I'm right.

"No, I mean, read it over and over and over, and possibly more after that until I get it perfect?"

"Sure, whatever you need," she says.

I return to my room and do what she suggested. I start from the beginning, short and sweet, to the point, and go from there. I type out a strong start without thinking: *When I was sixteen, I was a victim of a life-threatening car crash.* It seems dramatic, but it should do in the scale of things. I finish the speech with the same kind of short and snappy approach. Taking it to Mom to read, she makes a few edits for me so that it flows better and makes more sense for an audience. By the end of the afternoon, I'm happy enough. *This speech better be good.* I'm not getting up in front of a whole bar to tell a shit story about how depressing it is to have a brain injury.

* * *

Stepping onto the stage, I look down at my knee that showed so much weakness only a year ago, when I twisted it wrong while running on the stairs, trying something new. What if this turns out to be the same thing? What if it's something I try, thinking it will do me good, and then my weak-ass body gives out, and then I spend the next two years fixing it in physiotherapy? *Don't be ridiculous, Kamya. You're on a freaking stage, standing; you'll do fine! You know how to fucking stand.* I reach the microphone and look into the crowd, seeing familiar faces and strangers staring at me silently as if I'm the main event. Which I guess I sort of am. I start, trying my best to project my voice and not sound as small as I remember sounding in the hospital.

"When I was sixteen, I was the victim of a life-threatening car crash. I wasn't driving, and I was wearing my seatbelt. It was just one of those things that happen. I'm happy to say that I got the worst injuries from the crash, but that doesn't come without a price. I suffered from an internal brain bleed around the centre of my brain, among numerous other internal injuries. This was most evident in the fact that I was partially paralyzed on my left side. Since the brain injury was the cause, the connections in my brain had a chance to rewire themselves.

"After a few weeks in an induced coma, I started what would be life-long rehabilitation. Since then, I'm very proud to say that I have learned to walk again, run again, talk again, eat properly, and I have learned whole new approaches to learning. I welcomed help when it was available, and I took on a gentle course load that would allow me to focus on my studies, along with my ongoing rehab. With the help of many people, here at UPEI included, I'm now very close to being able to graduate with full credits. Since that day, I've learned much about the brain and the human body and how far determination can bring somebody."

I take a deep breath.

"I think the most important thing I learned during these past seven years is that everybody is different. Brains are unique to every person, just like how every person is unique to every society. Now, I don't remember how I learned this, and I don't remember if it was before my injuries or after. Still, I used this information to understand better what was happening to me. In the twenty-first century, humans, who are naturally smart beings, know very little about the brain. One thing is evident, though: this organ is the main contributor to the functioning of all other organs in the body. So, needless to say, my main issues were not simply present in my motor capabilities and my memory. My main issue was the influence my brain had on my life.

"I needed to preserve as much of myself as I possibly could. When the doctors told me there was a possibility that certain things might affect my brain negatively, I listened. When they told me to avoid alcohol, drugs, stress, and too much stimulation (such as screentime), I did just that. One of the benefits that I chose to add to my plan was meditation. I took a course in Transcendental Meditation, and now I routinely meditate for twenty minutes twice a day. This increased my sense of self-worth and self-awareness and dramatically helped with my fatigue. While understanding that everyone is different, I highly recommend mindfulness strategies to help anyone.

"I took all the advice given to me. I listened to it all in the best way I could. I took all that information and then applied my knowledge of how all brains differ. I found the best methods for me and continued using those. You can see as many professionals as possible, but all that monitored rehabilitation can only take you so far. They cannot possibly know you like you know you. For example, I figured out on my own that watching Disney movies was one of my most effective stress relievers."

As it says in my notes, I pause for laughter, and yet I'm surprised when it comes.

"Disney movies, to me, act as simple motivational moments. They act as comic relief and bring me back to a simpler time when I was just a little girl trying to sing along in the best pitch possible. They represent something special to me, and allow me to take a break from the stresses I may be dealing with in life. Knowing and applying your individuality is as necessary as learning the best-known management methods with the help of a professional. You need their support as much as you need your own. I may never be back to the person I was before my brain was affected, but I feel ready to take life on. I have learned from my experiences. I did it, and I know you can, too, no matter what life brings you.

"With every challenge or obstacle that we face in life, if we tackle one small thing at a time together and master it, the future doesn't look so scary. We can achieve that which we set out to achieve."

Suddenly I'm finished. The silence of my voice no longer amplified through the room is deafening for an instant, and then I get a big applause. Holding back my tears, I make it back to my seat. I did it! I'm not sure I made eye contact, but I don't care. I did it, and that's what matters.

Three more speakers follow me. I barely hear one because I'm still calming down from my speech—it's definitely better to be in the crowd than on the stage. One speaker is a girl younger than me who gives a fantastically moving speech about her brother and how he killed himself, putting her and her family into shock, and questioning everything. It's beautiful and makes me question if mine was even a fraction as powerful. Next is a middle-aged woman who experienced a brain injury in a crash not too different from mine. I can imagine it gives people two different perspectives on the same issue. Where I spoke about rehabilitation, she speaks of her mental health and how hard things have been on her and her family. It's stuff I didn't cover because, for me, it's the background noise of my rehabilitation, but that doesn't mean it's not essential. Not only do people experience things differently, but how we interpret them is entirely unique, too. There are so many factors to consider, which I guess was the point of my speech. My studies have consumed me, and now that they're soon finished, I have no idea what to do with my life.

At the end, all speakers gather on stage for the last applause. I want to thank the girl who shared the story about her brother.

"By the way," I whisper to her as we gather for a picture, "your speech was my favourite. I just want to thank you personally for coming up here and sharing that with us. It couldn't have been easy. Also, I'm so sorry about your brother."

"Oh," She says. I can tell she must be used to people giving her their regrets, just like I'm used to people's reactions to my brain injury. I can see that uncertainty of not knowing what to say back.

"It's okay," I say. "You don't have to say anything back to me. I know how it is."

She laughs. "But I do want to say something! You just kind of cornered me, is all. But I *absolutely loved* your speech as well. You're such an interesting person and really made the best out of a bad situation."

"So did you," I say. "Didn't you say that you and your parents now take part in suicide awareness? That's so significant. I imagine you're helping so many people."

"Yes, we are," she says. "It was such a tragedy. We all feel like we should have seen it coming. Now that we're more educated about it, I wonder if we would see it now."

"I don't know, people are so good at being secretive," I say, thinking about how many secrets I keep from people, even my mom. "And sometimes, they might not know themselves until it happens."

"You're right," she says, and we quickly pose for the camera.

"I'm so sorry," I quickly add. "Would it be okay if I hugged you? I'm told I'm pretty good at hugging, and I just want to thank you so much for all you do."

"Of course. I'd love that." As we embrace, she adds, "I love being in a group of these kinds of people. It feels so nice just to be accepted and understood so easily."

I think of how much one person can affect another simply by accepting them and creating connections. My brain injury has helped me understand people more deeply, after all—understand that people all have their own problems and that no one is necessarily better or worse than any other. As members of the same species, we should support and welcome each other, not separate ourselves into different groups and labels.

Maybe this is what I'll do. Support people and individuals to help them understand that they're not alone. In some sort of mushed-up, spaghetti-like way, we're all connected. We can spend years separating ourselves with labels or diagnoses, but it doesn't change reality. We *can* help one another. We *can* have similarities and familial bonds. We *can* make a difference. I'm not sure how yet, but this is it. Connecting with others and making them feel less alone. This is what I want to do with my life. Maybe I can become a counsellor. Maybe I'll finally write that book Mom first encouraged me to write. I'm not sure how I'll make money from it; I'm not even sure if I want to. Maybe a career isn't what I'm seeking, but as far as what I want to do in life, *this is it!*

Back at home, I finally approach Mom and do what I never thought I'd be able to do— I ask for her neon-orange notebook.

Epilogue

First, I want to thank you for reading my story. I hope you got something out of it, but if you didn't, that's okay, too. This is a story of growth: the good, the bad, and the truthful. It's a story for those experiencing traumatic moments in their lives and for their loved ones so that they can better understand what might be going on inside their head without having to ask. Remember that everyone experiences trauma differently and that not everyone has internal dialogue like I do in this story. I'm not aiming to be a saint; I only wanted to demonstrate my process, the tolls taken, and the lessons learned. I'll admit that I'm a work in progress, and there's always room for growth.

My storytelling isn't perfect, either. I used certain people to show how our older populations think because they were my best representations at the time. My memories don't often come to me all at once in a linear fashion, and when they do, it's almost impossible to tell what's real. Most come to me when an unknown trigger sneaks up and reminds me of a particular day, physical memory, or emotion. Over time, these memories became repetitive, often coming to me when I was most rested, and my brain was relaxed. These memories are the ones I've stuck to, in order to write this book. While perhaps not always correct, this is the order my brain sorted them out to make a beginning, middle, and end for myself.

The entire first three chapters and into the fourth are made-up memories devised from my mom's orange notebook and stories told to me repeatedly. I spent so much time without those memories that I very vividly recreated them on my own, helping with the loss it gave me. The story of my first steps, where my brother is the one to encourage me to get up, is my mom's favourite; however, I've always imagined it going differently in my head, and wrote it as such. I have zero memory of the accident itself, but I wrote how it replays in my head when I think of it unwillingly.

In reality, I believe my first true recalled memories start around the drive back to PEI or my birthday in the hospital. When I wrote about Mom surprising me with a hospital version of ham and scalloped potatoes or when Kristy visited me, memories started fragmenting and feeling like my own. However, I couldn't add the input of my cousin, who worked as staff in the hospital kitchen then and had helped her make that breakfast happen for me. I wasn't aware of these occurrences then, so I wrote it that way. I tried to write the story this way as much as possible. The help I received from not only friends and family but also other Islanders and the professionals around me was enormous.

After much debate, I kept my name, but changed all others except for the locations and celebrities because, frankly, if I was going to change one name, I was going to change them all. Some changes were intentional, such as the mental health week at UPEI that I participated in. I wrote it as happening at the time of my graduation when in reality it was the year before. I had to change the speech to fit into the story, but most of it was the one I gave on that stage. It's this moment that I still see as a representation of my graduation, and so I wrote it as such.

In hindsight, how it happened doesn't seem as important anymore. It's how I remember it that matters to me.

Now for a quick recap: I graduated from university in 2016 with a 2.9 GPA that spring. I don't really understand how that is calculated, considering my first three years have no GPA score that I can see, but it doesn't matter to me. I now live independently and feel confident that I graduated from university.

My relationship with Adam didn't work out, but that's okay. This story wasn't about romantic love. The knowledge and experiences I gained are how I treasure this time. The following fall, my mom and I took a trip to Malta to celebrate graduation with my friend Elena, whom I met in my psychology class. Our graduation trip plans remained intact and I'm so happy for that. We followed our celebrations with a week in the Dolomites of Italy with her wonderful family. We were so effortlessly welcomed into her family that they were family by the end of our trip. We were in Italy when they announced that Donald Trump would be president.

By late winter 2020, the coronavirus had reached North America and was starting to make history. From the cushioned shores of Prince Edward Island, we sat in terror as cases and death numbers rose and governments shut down. Eventually, it hit our shores, but I'm happy to say later than most. Having gone through such terrifying times, I believe that it will undoubtedly change everyone's future. When you experience the end of something, it helps you realize the impact of change. Still, you can change in your desired direction with effort, a little stubborness, and a touch of gumption. These times highlight the importance of being there for one another and the importance of the little things.

Small things were some of the most impactful for me and my story. No longer being able to drink coffee or alcohol, no late nights with friends, no long strenuous hikes to burn off energy, nothing to help me escape my life and help me feel "normal." I eventually found meditation, but I didn't mention those small things enough to do justice to how much agony it gave me. It sounds silly to be unable to do normal things with your friends because you get tired at seven o'clock. Still, the constant fear of addiction, fatigue, and tomorrow's energy levels can easily take away that feeling of normalcy. Even though I yearned for that feeling, I kept them out of reach. In the end, though, it was worth it. For as many small things that hurt my heart, body, and soul, there were as many small things that lifted them, helped me regain my sense of self, and made me feel welcome in the world. Doctors told Mom and James about the benefits of music therapy while I was in my coma—that's why they played music for me. Still, I never really felt the effects of music until years later when I was trying to find my continued inspiration. Small moments with a movie, a song, or with a stranger, those moments help even out the world and level a balance.

Being there for one another, recognizing our similarities, and living in harmony are just some things different groups, such as Indigenous Canadians, have tried to teach future generations. While I can't speak for these communities, I must give them that credit. If only we could learn from other communities rather than push them aside because they are different. I believe we could have the opportunity to grow, be unique, and unite all simultaneously.

I still believe everyone has difficulties in life and that they're vastly different between individuals; however, I'll also recognize that I'm probably very naive in naming it so simply. Not every brain or body injury is the same. I lost a fraction of my brain and temporarily lost the ability to do simple things. It took me months to regain my actual physical smile through electrotherapy. Still, I gained most of those abilities back while others might not have been able to. Even with the support, love, and optimism that I had access to, it was still so hard. Imagine what it could have been like alongside other problems, like being estranged from one's family or having people deny you access to help. Imagine not having the chance to regain these abilities. What if my mother wasn't there to help me through it all? What if I didn't have insurance to help cover the losses? I often ask myself questions like these, not to victimize others but to better understand them and myself.

While I didn't visit a psychologist around my graduation, I highly recommend others do so when going through difficult times or trying to sort out their lives. Before the publication of this book, though, I did start seeing a trauma counsellor. It took longer than it should have to realize these things about myself. I only learned while reading a draft of this book that I blamed a lot of outside factors for my emotional trauma. Now, I believe my trauma was from the complete experience, its intensity, and the toll it took on me to come to terms with my new originality. It was just the overwhelming smack of reality that I experienced all in a short amount of time. I understand now that my inability to see a psychologist was not that seeing a psychologist is scary or unnecessary. It was only one of the associations I made for myself in the events that followed my brain injury.

Finding a "new normal" isn't just a Covid term. It's also an oversimplified explanation of what change can force. It can dramatically and permanently alter your everyday life, forcing you to find a new living pattern that fits you better. Of course, you can try to resist, but that only postpones the inevitable. Finding a new normal shouldn't be scary. It should be seen as an opportunity to adapt and find comfort. You want to *feel* normal, which can lead you to try and recreate a time and feeling of comfort, but that doesn't necessarily mean returning to your old life. My own body often gives up on me when I just want to step forward with no thought or worry that I'll hurt myself; when I can't do that, it will always feel like self-betrayal. I remind myself way too often of the biological structure of my mind and human body, of the battles I've gone through, and of the good things in life. I don't punish myself anymore for feeling those feelings. If I need a minute or two to give myself that outlet of emotions, I do. There's not much else I can do or say. It's just what I've gotten used to, and it's my new normal; not normal for everyone else, but normal for me.

Acknowledgements

The first person I would like to thank is, of course, my mom, to whom I dedicated this book. She's been my strength through it all, both physically and emotionally and just by how she raised me. She's forever my rock, and because of her I was able to have moments where I could break down because I always knew she'd be there for me if I needed help to be built back up. Not to mention that this book was her idea, and even though she gave me the idea way before I was ready, I think it's been in the back of my mind since then. Not long after I graduated, I was able to gain independence. That's how I wrote this book that many have since asked for. This includes a stranger that I met only once while working in tourism on PEI who, after a brief conversation, told me I'd make a good author. I assured him then that I was working on it, and I'd love to thank him now for that little bit of encouragement whether he finds himself reading this or not. I remember a conversation with Mom around the time I was in the finishing stages of my book, where I told her I was afraid to make my story public. She asked, "Why? When was the last time you cared what anyone thought of you?" and it hit me. She was right; I've learned to believe that if the people who know the most about brains still can't map out what makes a perfect person, then who am I trying to be?

I want to thank my brother, who's always been there for me, acting as my connection to the outside world. Even though there were times when he made me cry as a kid, he was my first friend, and he will forever be. I want to thank my dad, who, even though it was difficult, took the time to give me my space when I needed it and then found his way back to me again when I needed it. I know he'd do anything for me, and I feel his love daily. Thanks also to Grammie, who shows me so much love and understanding and makes the best lunches for me on days when I might have a therapy appointment, even to this day. All my friends, including the ones who helped me edit this book, thank you. I've always been fortunate to find the most beautiful friends in the world—people I can be myself with, not worry about, and who would always have my back in every situation. Friends are truly gold on Earth; I don't know where I'd be without them. The medical professionals and registered therapists I've worked with, who have helped me find the best ways to rehabilitate, ones that best suited me as an individual and helped me through some of my most difficult times: your work is most powerful, and I'm here to remind you that you certainly make a difference. People who write and perform music and work in the entertainment industry, including the ones I mentioned in this book, you have the potential to make a huge difference in the world. Sometimes, I wonder if you know how much of an impact you have when I'm alone, crying in my bedroom with nothing but your art to comfort me. Moments when my mom and I watched daytime TV to relax and unwind from our stressful days, or when I watch movies to detangle my brain and forget the world around me—they might seem silly, but quiet moments like those, where we can feel ordinary or included laughing alongside celebrities, can help us get from one day to the next.

The friendly Islanders and tourists with whom I live my everyday life also need to be thanked. We have the power to impact each person's day, and I love people who recognize this and choose to use their power for good, day in and day out. Tourists who visit and are happy to share their experiences and gratitude: I value our interactions. I'd like to thank the people I interacted with at UPEI during my years there. My experiences on that campus will stay with me for the rest of my life. I hope the small stories I wrote can help people understand that even the smallest interactions can be powerful. People in my life who were pivotal in allowing me to have a good day, where I felt seen and loved even when sitting alone. To my dogs at home and my aunt's dogs, whom I spent time with while studying: they knew when to be quiet and when to come to me looking for love and attention. Finally, I want to thank the Traumatic Brain Injury Support Group on Facebook. I only discovered you while writing this book. Still, even years after my TBI, I've found comfort in relating to others who've had similar experiences. I definitely encourage joining support groups wherever you can find them and seeking people who can understand your frustration and make you feel less alone.

In 2020, we learned firsthand how vital our essential workers are during the COVID-19 pandemic. Across generations, we've increased value on more educated jobs, seeing more essential jobs become diminished in social worth. When it became apparent that we needed them, essential workers were celebrated in the streets. Not long after, when the world slowly began opening up again, allowing people to return to the office, our so-called essential workers were forgotten. Suddenly, they weren't worth the pay raise or extra time off, even though they had to work overtime to care for us when we needed them most. I want to tell you that you're still seen, and I aim for a future where you can be more respected for your hard work.

FORGET REGRET

Remember, every one of us is influential in each other's lives. We need to recognize this and show each other our appreciation.

Playlist

- "Upside Down" by Jack Johnson (January, 2001)
- "Fields of Gold" by Celtic Woman (January, 2009)
- "Galway Bay" by Celtic Woman (January, 2007)
- "When You Believe" by Celtic Woman (January, 2009)
- "True Colors" by Cyndi Lauper (September, 1986)
- "Danny Boy" by Frederic Weatherly (1918)
- "Raise a Little Hell" by Trooper (March, 1979)
- "Benny And The Jets" by Elton John (October, 1973)
- "Sorry Seems to Be the Hardest Word" by Elton John (October, 1976)
- "If I Die Young" by The Band Perry (January, 2010)
- "Your Song" by Elton John (November, 2018)
- "Temporary Home" by Carrie Underwood (November, 2009)
- "Fight Song" by Rachel Platten (February, 2015)

www.ingramcontent.com/pod-product-compliance
Lightning Source LLC
LaVergne TN
LVHW040047080526
838202LV00045B/3534